sadhu sundar singh

sadhu sundar singh

CYRIL J. DAVEY

BEACON HILL PRESS OF KANSAS CITY
KANSAS CITY, MISSOURI

First published 1950 by SCM Press
Reprinted by special arrangement with
SCM Press, LTD., London, England
First printing of this edition, 1968
Second printing, 1992

ISBN: 083-411-4356

Printed in the
United States of America

Cover Design: Crandall Vail

10   9   8   7   6   5   4   3   2

Contents

YEAR OF DISCIPLESHIP

We cannot tell what we do not know. The more we know, the better we will respond through prayer, giving, and answering God's call for involvement in mission ministry.

The **Year of Discipleship** presents a special challenge to be mission-minded. **Every individual and congregation is urged to renew their commitment to the value of mission education.** Andrew Murray appropriately stated, "[Mission] information is the fuel without which the fire cannot burn. Fuel is not fire . . . fuel is indispensable to keep the fire burning. An informed church will be a transformed church" *(Key to the Missionary Problem).*

Failure to be informed about world missions through systematic study and reading often invokes such questions as "Why world mission?" "Why send missionaries?" "Why General Budget?" Since the knowledge of world mission does not come through firsthand experience for most of us, it is important that there be a system for receiving mission information.

The Church of the Nazarene provides such a system through the mission education arm of NWMS. Resource (study) packets are produced annually for adults, youth, and children. The study materials contain planned lessons on guided tracks and are enriched with visuals and presentation ideas for large or small groups of any size church. There are reading books for all age levels, as well as slides, videos, and films; and *World Mission* magazine is published monthly. All of the resources help develop a mission-minded person and church.

The individuals or churches who best fulfill the Great Commission of our Lord Jesus Christ to "Go . . . make disciples" know who they are, where they are, and what their needs and biblical responsibilities are. Mission education helps a person understand his responsibility to God's world.

What is the **purpose** of mission education? It is to give information consistent with the biblical basis of the Great Commission and, in the Church of the Nazarene, to interface biblical truth with the needs and victories of **Nazarene missions.** We learn that which develops us in the faith . . . that effects change in our thinking and behavior . . . that effects change for all eternity in the lives of those in the uttermost parts of the world.

Learn . . . **Go!**

—NINA G. GUNTER
General NWMS Director

Preface

Perhaps no country on the face of the earth offers more in the way of challenge and intrigue than India. From the towering Himalayan mountains on the north, to the Indian Ocean on the south, its over 800 million people now constitute the second most populated nation on earth. By the year 2020, however, India is projected to surpass China and become the world's most populated country.

India is a myriad of sociological, political, religious, educational, and economic contrasts. Its people speak more than 1,600 different languages and dialects, with 14 different "official" languages existing. India is known as the world's largest functioning democracy, but regional, caste, and religious loyalties often break out in devastating violence and destructiveness. Over 80% of India's peoples are Hindu and 11% are Muslim, making India the world's third largest Muslim country. Barely 3% of the population can be classified "Christian," with less than 1% evangelical Christians.

India. What a place of enormous challenge and spiritual need.

The struggle to light the fires of Christian truth in India has continued across many decades, as evidenced by the biography in this book. A great price has been paid by those who have committed themselves to this objective.

India is one of the first countries where the Church of the Nazarene commenced its missionary effort. When the Church of the Nazarene came into existence in 1908, there were three different groups receiving support in India from those that formed the new denomination. Across the years this has grown until today India is one of the most exciting areas of growth in our entire world family. There are five districts and over 35,000 Nazarenes. The 1991 growth rate exceeded 14%! Every district and local church is led by Indian Nazarenes, as is the outstanding Reynolds Memorial Nazarene Hospital located in Washim, north central India.

I have seen no greater examples of holy living, of Nazarene loyalty, or of evangelistic fervor anywhere in the world than I have seen in India. Recently I spent a week speaking in an all-India pastors' conference held on the campus of our Nazarene Bible College in Washim. The scores of men and women who sat daily in those services and voiced their love for God and church, and their commitment to evangelize India, inspired me as I have seldom been inspired.

Sadhu Sundar Singh was truly an early saint of India. The truth is, however, there are many more such saints in today's India. Through their Churches of the Nazarene they bear sacrificial witness to their love for Jesus Christ, and to their determination to help His kingdom come to their great and needy country.

As you read this book, may you breathe the prayer for 21st-century saints to continue to walk India's dusty roads and busy streets. Jesus is the answer. The Church of the Nazarene will help make that answer known to the millions of India.

ROBERT H. SCOTT
World Mission Director

By way of explanation:

Sadhu is a designation given to a holy man in India.

Sundar was the given name of the subject of this story.

Singh (pronounced "sing") is the surname of every Sikh ("seek") family. It is their word for "lion." Sundar's father's name was Sher Singh.

Preface to First Edition

Firsthand material for the life of Sadhu Sundar Singh is not easy to discover, for, though he left an ineffaceable memory with many people, he wrote little himself. He published a few books dealing with the spiritual life, but he hardly ever kept a journal or diary of his wanderings. For accounts of his adventures one must turn to his two principal biographers or to the illustrations he used in his sermons and addresses. It is not always easy to decide whether these references deal with actual happenings or whether they are the result of some strange mystical experiences. Those who knew him best interpret his words in different ways.

Mrs. Arthur Parker's *Sadhu Sundar Singh—Called of God* was published during the Sadhu's lifetime and by his permission. C. F. Andrews' *Sadhu Sundar Singh—A Personal Memoir*, published four years after his death, is the result of a long friendship and probably no one has ever penetrated so deeply into the sadhu's way of thinking. These two books will remain as standard sources for his life story. In addition, Dr. Streeter and Dr. Appaswamy in *The Sadhu* and Dr. Heiler of Marburg in *The Gospel of Sadhu Sundar Singh* provide most useful assessments of his religious experience and teaching.

The sadhu's own writings are mainly meditations and transcriptions of addresses. The best known are *Visions of the Spiritual World, Reality and Religion, The Spiritual Life, The Search After Reality*, and *With and Without Christ*.

1

1896

The Sadhu in the Jungle

Sundar wiped the sweat from his eyes and wondered if his mother did not notice the heat.

He wound his white turban cloth round his nose and mouth, so that he should not breathe the fine yellow dust that his mother's sandals whipped up into clouds as they trudged across the Punjab plain. It had been hot enough among the houses of Rampur village, where Sundar lived; but here in the open desert the morning sun burned through the child's copper-colored skin. Above them the sky was steely blue, turning gray at the distant horizon. The only considerable vegetation other than the trees around the wells or those marking the distant road was a tangled jungle of scrubby undergrowth and tall trees where hidden springs irrigated the ground. These alone broke the level monotony of the plain.

Toward this jungle the boy and his mother were tramping. It was no new experience. Ever since he was a baby, when his mother carried him on her hip, he had made this fortnightly journey to the holy man who lived among the trees. In a village where there was no calendar it marked the passage of time, as did the other visit to present flowers at the Hindu shrine just outside Rampur village. Today, however, the journey was different. His skin began to prickle from excitement as well as from the sudden cold-

13

ness of the trees as they at last entered the shade of the jungle.

Today was his seventh birthday.

And he was going to recite the *Gita* to the holy man.

The *Gita* was not his own sacred book, for he was a Sikh, and in the Sikh temples the *Granth Sahib*, the book written 400 years ago, lay on its silken cushions. But the *Gita* is treasured throughout India, Hindu book though it is. Sundar's mother believed that God spoke in many ways, and in every faith, and taught her son the same way of thinking. As soon as he could speak he learned by heart the prayers of his own people, and when he could listen without his baby mind being distracted by the lizards that ran up the mud walls of the houses, it was stories from the sacred scriptures that he heard. Soon he began to learn them himself, and before long he could recite many of them in the very words his mother used. Then it was that she began to teach him the long chapters of the *Gita*. Full of unfamiliar names, poetry, and theological argument as it was, he could hardly understand it when he had learned it. Yet, despite this, he loved it.

They stepped across the fallen pipal [fig] tree, moved round the bend of the path where a grass snake wriggled almost under their feet, and up the narrow track on the left. Sundar looked for the holy man, the sadhu, and found him sitting in the spot where he had sat as long as the boy could remember. Though he had lived in the forest for a score of years, no one knew anything about his history—only that he had gone into the forest to be alone with God. Sometimes such sadhus had a mad look in their eyes; often they had mutilated their bodies, closing their fists till their nails grew through their palms, or refusing to use the right arm until at last it was shriveled and dead through disuse. Generally they were dirty, their hair tangled, and their skin smeared with ashes. This holy man was different. His body was clean; his eyes were clear; his yellow robe (the color that every sadhu wears) was washed, though it was now faded to a drab tan. He was ready to talk with those who sought him and would not parade his holiness under a mysterious, unbreakable silence.

The mother led Sundar to him, and they spoke together. He smiled at the boy and asked him questions, his old eyes lighting up with pleasure at the child's answers. Then, commanding him to recite what he knew of the *Gita*, the sadhu sat still and waited.

In a sharp treble, Sundar began his long recitation.

After a while the old man held up his hand. "You have done well, boy." Sundar felt his body glow and throb with pleasure at such unlikely praise. Then the old voice spoke again: "But you are too proud at having done it. Pride is our deadly enemy. Learn the *Gita*, boy, yes . . . but learn humility too. It is the path that leads to God."

Sundar dropped his eyes. The old man was right. He *was* proud. He listened as the saint spoke again:

"What does the *Gita* tell us of the way to please God, child?"

"The way to please Him is to keep every law, every tradition that has been handed down by our fathers . . ."

"Is there no other way?"

"Yes, *sadhuji*. The way of meditation, of self-denial, the way of the sadhu—to cut oneself off from the world of men and think only of the things of God."

The old man under the tree looked pleased. He gave the mother a calm smile.

"The boy speaks well," he told her. She dropped her eyes in a gesture of humility. "Who knows," he went on, "but that the day will come when he may be a sadhu himself."

Sundar walked back across the desert with the words ringing in his ears, unaware, now, that the sun was hotter than ever.

At home, however, there was another opinion, and his father had no hesitation in expressing it. Sirdar Sher Singh was tall, vigorous, and black-bearded, with the air of a man accustomed to being obeyed. There was no arrogance about him, for among the Sikhs all men are spiritual equals; but he was nevertheless the *Sirdar,* the landowner and chieftain of this part of Patiala State. His relatives were in the maharajah's service, wealthy landowners like himself, or were to become known as high-ranking lawyers and soldiers. The time would come when Sundar, with his older brother, would inherit his position. Too much religion would not help him when that day came.

Sher Singh was not opposed to religion or its exercises. The Sikhs take their religion seriously, and Sher Singh, a devout man himself, was proud that his wife, Sundar's mother, was honored as a *bhakta,* a woman saint, throughout the district. What worried him was that she seemed determined to make young Sundar a saint before his time. The boy rose as early as his mother, recited prayers in the worship room at her side, and was not allowed even a glass of milk until the household devotions were finished.

"There's plenty of time for prayers," said his father. "Go off and play games with the other boys."

Sundar, who never questioned his father's orders, obediently went to join the boys outside the *gurdwara* (the temple). But before long he deserted the game and wandered into the temple itself to listen to the priest reading the *Granth Sahib.*

"*He* will never make a warrior," lamented a graybeard who could remember the Emperor Maharaj Singh and who had fought against the British at Chilianwala in the days of the great Sikh Empire.

The Sikhs have been soldiers since the days in the 18th century when persecution nearly wiped them out completely. The religious leader, the *guru,* of that day organized them into a martial brotherhood, gave every man the surname of "Singh" (lion), ordered them to fight to the death for the honor of their race, and gave them certain signs of their brotherhood that all might recognize. They were not to hide themselves, looking like other men. No Sikh may shave his beard or cut his hair; he must wear the steel bracelet and carry the *kirpan,* the short, sharp dagger that proclaims his courage.

Sundar knew these things and recalled them with pride. He longed for the day when he would have a beard as black and thick as his father's, and would stride, a 6-foot giant, about the state town of Patiala. None loved the Sikh race more dearly than he did. He thrilled at the stories of martyrdom that many of his ancestors had undergone rather than betray the brotherhood. But, at the same time, he could never forget that they were a *religious* brotherhood, a nation founded on a sacred book. He remembered that the earliest teachers had gone on missionary journeys across India, Ceylon, Burma, even to the borders of closed Tibet itself.

Was there no way to combine these things? The military valor, the courage of the martyrs, the adventures of the missionary preachers, the pride of race, the devoutness of the saints . . . The words of the holy man challenged him again and again. ". . . a sadhu himself, perhaps!"

"He will become either a saint or a fool," mumbled Sher Singh's cronies as they watched the chieftain's son slip into the temple.

Sher Singh, knowing it was useless to talk to his wife about his anxieties for the boy, spoke to his own priest instead. The priest looked the black-bearded Sirdar full in the eye.

"I don't know what to make of the boy," he answered. "He is not like the rest of them." Then he spoke words that Sher Singh never forgot. "He will become a great man someday—if he does not disgrace us all by going mad."

17

2

1903

The Burning of the Book

"The boy is growing fast," Sher Singh agreed with his friends, but he looked troubled when Jaswant Singh commented that he would be a credit to the family.

"I trust he may be." The landowner went on after a pause: "He has no taste for arms, and too much conscience to succeed at the bar or in the service of the state."

"He goes less to the temple these days," put in Ram Singh.

"And not so often to the sadhu in the jungle with his mother."

"It is not because he would not, but because his schooling interferes. But make no mistake, it does not curb his devotions. You will find him in the prayer room each morning with his mother before he goes to the mission school."

"Is it good for him, do you think," queried Jaswant Singh, "to go to the Christian school?"

"Never fear, friend. Sundar is a Sikh. He is proud of his inheritance. They will never make a Christian of him."

"The Christian teachers come to your house, Sher Singh."

"True. His mother is a *bhakta*, as you well know, and seeks truth wherever she may find it. I am no great hand at religious matters—I take the word of the *guru* for the things I must believe—but I know that our own teachers have told us that God reveals himself in many ways, that many voices and many books speak of Him. . . ."

"Even the Christian Book, which they learn in the Christian school?"

"Perhaps. I do not read it, Jaswant Singh. To listen to the priest reading in the temple is enough for me. And Sundar does not read it either. The Christian Book makes him strangely angry. He bought a little part of their Book once but had read only a page or two when he tore it apart and threw it away, swearing never to read it again or listen to its being taught."

"Then why does he go to the Christian school?"

"Because the government school is three miles away, as you well know; too far to walk each day in the heat of the plains. He *must* have schooling somewhere if he is to get on in the world!" Sher Singh rose, leaning heavily on a stick, for he was lame in one leg. "I confess I do not like so much religion in a boy of 12, but at least it is the faith for which our fathers suffered martyrdom that he loves. And the *Granth Sahib* of our people he cherishes, though he knows the Hindu and Islamic scriptures by heart." He limped away from the trees toward his house.

Jaswant Singh looked at the graybearded Ram Singh, lying where the shadows of the pipal leaves deepened the dark brown of his lined face. "Sher Singh loves his son well, but he will never know what to make of him, Brother!"

It was true enough that Sher Singh loved his son. How could anyone help it? Courage and honesty shone brightly in brown eyes much like his mother's, and they were qualities that every Sikh held dear. But, because he was his mother's son as much as his father's, his resoluteness was matched by an urgent compassion for those in need.

Sometimes love and honesty came into conflict, as on the occasion when he found a dying beggar woman in the bazaar. He begged for food and clothing for her from his father, who refused because his gates would be besieged with malarial beggars. Pity drove Sundar to steal a 10-rupee note from his father's money, but on the way to the bazaar honesty sent him back to return it. He found the theft was discovered and fear made him blame the servants, who were beaten, but conscience forced him to waken Sher Singh at midnight and confess. Sher Singh praised his honesty and courage and sent him back to bed. He would rather have been beaten too.

The world collapsed for Sundar when he was near 14, for his mother died. It was from her that all his spiritual strength had been drawn. When he read the holy books, he could hear her voice repeating the sacred words; when he prayed in the morning, she was by his side; when he visited the sadhu under the pipal tree, he trod in her sandal prints. She was for him, more than any other, the way to God. When she died, Sundar was literally desperate. He knew that he could not live without God, and yet the one person who could make God real to him God himself had taken away. He read the words of the Sikh teachers over again: "I cannot live for a moment without Thee, my Lord"; "I long for Thee; I thirst for Thee; only in Thee does my heart find rest." As he spoke the urgent phrases, he hardly knew whether they referred to God or to his mother. No one in the world could ever mean so much to him again.

To the end of his life he spoke of her with passionate affection. Whatever he was, he owed first to her. No man, he declared, was ever truly good who had not a good mother. Many years later he was to sit in the study of the arch-bishop of Canterbury and assert that so sure was he of her love of God that if he came to heaven and found she was not there he would ask God that he might be sent to hell to bear her comfort. No one could serve God as she did, and not find her way to His presence.

Sundar was desolate. His father could say nothing to help him, for he, too, was stricken with grief. The holy man to whom they went together gave him no peace, nor did the *guru* in the village temple. For a few months Sundar tried ineffectually to practice the way of disciplined meditation known as *yoga*. The kindness of his Christian teachers at school was even worse. He hated them, their school, their Scriptures, and their Jesus.

Suddenly he altered. From a peaceful, courteous, devout schoolboy he changed into a violent young ruffian. He alternated between a longing for spiritual peace and a violent resentment against God. When his Christian teachers suggested that Jesus Christ, whom they served, would give him the peace he yearned for, they set the spark to his smoldering hatred for all they represented.

For a little while he contented himself with interrupting rudely in class, asking absurd and irrelevent questions, and walking out of the room after abusing the teachers when the Scripture period arrived. He refused to read or listen to the New Testament. So viciously did he rebel against the Christian faith that he persuaded his father to take him away from the school and allow him to tramp the six miles across the Punjab desert to the government school each day.

Free of the control of the mission school, he could show his hatred of it more plainly. He gathered together a group of young hooligans from the bazaar, boys whom he had hitherto despised as dirty and evil, and made himself their leader. Sundar was bent on more than schoolboy pranks. He was determined to break up the Christian school and drive the missionaries and the little band of Christians who lived in the bazaar out of town. With his gang, he maliciously stoned the preachers in the bazaar, flung dirt and ordure into the Christian meetings, and shouted down those who protested. No one could credit that this rowdy rascal was the quiet boy who had gone to the temple week after week with his mother. Sher Singh listened, almost unbelieving, to the tales he heard of his son's evildoing. The Christian teachers put the kindest construction they could on his actions and decided he was temporarily out of his mind with grief.

No one understood that Sundar, who had claimed that he longed for the peace of God, was taking this way of fighting against God.

The summer dragged on, hotter and hotter, until Sundar lost all his anger and energy as he tramped across the hot sand to his new school. In the end he could do it no longer. He fell sick with malaria and, in the depression that followed the fever, agreed wearily that his father should try to get him readmitted to the American Presbyterian School in Rampur. The teachers whom he had stoned and maltreated agreed, without much enthusiasm, to take him back.

They found him quieter. His violence had spent itself, leaving only an intense depression. There were days when he wished that he could die. He gave little attention to his lessons, sitting listlessly as others asked or answered questions. The only time he seemed to come to life was in the Scripture classes, when he sidetracked the lesson with shrewd comments on the absurdity of the Christian story, or fatuous questions that roused the class to laughter at the teacher's expense.

His 14th birthday had passed when Sundar went back to the mission school. The last of the hot weather died away in October, and November had gone when Sundar suddenly asked the schoolmaster to sell him a copy of the New Testament. The teacher's heart quickened. It seemed that the moment they had prayed for had come. He told his colleagues what he had done as Sundar left the school. Their rejoicing would have ceased very quickly had they heard what Sundar was saying to his friends.

"Come with me. You are surprised that I should buy this Book, but come home and see what I do with it! How long I shall live I cannot tell you. Not long, certainly; but before I die I will show you what I think of Jesus and His Book!"

Sundar led the way into the courtyard.

His companions waited, watching curiously as he came from the kitchen carrying a bundle of sticks and a tin of kerosene oil. They moved to help him make his fire, but he waved them away. It was his own last gesture of contemptuous hatred that they were to see. He poured the oil on the wood and set a match to it. It flared brightly in the shadows by the wall. Then he took from his pocket the New Testament and began, slowly and methodically, to tear it to pieces, leaf by leaf, letting each page burn to ashes before he put the next on the flames.

Suddenly his father walked out of the house. He glanced at his son, at the Book in his hand, and at the charred paper on the fire.

"Are you mad, child?" he thundered. "Are you beside yourself to burn the Christians' Book? It is a good Book—your mother has said so—and I will not have this evildoing in my house. Stop it, do you hear! *Stop it!*"

Sundar looked at his father. He did not notice his friends slipping silently out of the courtyard. Swiftly he bent down, thrust the rest of the New Testament into the fire, pressed it into the heart of the fierce fire with his foot, and entered the house without a word.

3

December 3, 1903

The Vision

The burning of the Book was to be Sundar's last gesture against God before he died. If God would not save, then he repudiated God. For months since his mother's death he had been searching for peace and could find none. The period of despair had come to an end. Cold, bitter resolution filled his heart.

For three days and nights he stayed in his room.

"If God wants me to live, let Him say so!

"O God, if there be a God, reveal thyself to me tonight."

His mind must be clear for what lay ahead. There must be no sleep, no dreaming. For a little while he stood silently. Not far away, on the main line, he heard the sound of a train. For three days he had known what he was going to do. This was no sudden, mad decision; it was the result of deliberate, calm meditation. The whistle sounded louder as the last train of the night rushed towards Lahore and was gone. The next express went through Rampur at five o'clock in the morning.

And if God had not spoken to him before that time, he would go out to the railway line, lay his head on the rails, and wait in the darkness for the train from Ludhiana to Lahore to end his misery.

He left the house and went out to the bathing room. In the chill of the evening he let the cold water pour over his head, his shoulders, his slim body. He bathed in the cold water for an hour before he returned to his room.

There were seven hours yet before the train was due.

"O God, if there be a God, reveal thyself before I die."

The hours passed.

Outside, the moon rose clear and white in the winter sky; a pack of jackals raced past the house, screaming in the still air. The howl of a hyena broke the silence. Sundar heard nothing. He sat, motionless, on the floor, with only the endless drumming of the express wheels in his mind.

The moon swung slowly across the sky.

It was a quarter to five when Sundar's door opened and he rushed out. He turned toward his father's room, went in, and seized the sleeping man by the shoulder.

Sher Singh leaped from his bed, flinging the blanket aside, and almost falling on his lame leg, clutched the boy's shoulder.

"What is the matter, boy?"

Sundar's reply jerked him into wakefulness.

"I have seen Jesus!"

Sher Singh sat down on the bed, watching the moonlight playing on his son's face. "You're dreaming, child. Go back to bed!"

"I am not dreaming." Sundar explained quietly how he had determined to end his life that night unless something happened.

"But something did happen. A few minutes ago Jesus came into my room. As I was praying for the last time a bright cloud of light suddenly filled the room—no, it was no trick of the moon—and out of the brightness came the face and figure of Jesus. He spoke to me. . . ."

"Spoke to you?"

"He said, *'How long wilt you persecute Me? I have come to save you. You were praying to know the right way; why do you not take it? I am the Way.'* He spoke in Hindustani, and He spoke to *me.* I fell at His feet. How long I knelt I cannot say. But as

I rose the vision faded. It *was* a vision. It was no thought of mine that called Him there. I had bathed. I was not thinking of Him or desiring Him. Had it been Krishna, or one of my own gods, I might have expected it—but not Jesus." He paused, while his father looked at him as though he were mad. Then he spoke again:

"I am a Christian. I can serve no one else but Jesus!"

Sher Singh spoke quietly, without anger or scorn. "You are half asleep, boy." Yet he knew as he looked that no one had ever been farther from sleep than Sundar at that moment. "Or else you have gone mad. Go back to bed." He led the boy to the door of the room. As Sundar moved slowly from it, Sher Singh spoke sharply:

"You *must* be mad. You come in the middle of the night and say you are a Christian—and yet it is not three days past that you burned the Christian Book!"

Sundar stood rigid, looking at his hands.

"These hands did it. I can never cleanse them of that sin till the day I die." He turned to his father. "But till that day comes my life is His."

4

1904-6

Persecution

Sher Singh tried, the next morning, to avoid any open clash with his 14-year-old son. In India, family loyalty is a high virtue. For Sundar to oppose his father would be unthinkable, but for Sher Singh loyalty to the *Khalsa,* the Sikh nation, outweighed even parental affections. He hoped the boy would admit he had been dreaming and, when he refused, adopted other tactics. Why should he not remain a secret disciple of Jesus while observing the outward ways of his own faith? asked Sher Singh. Had not his mother found some of the truth in every religion?

Sundar refused to accept such a subterfuge. He could not have maintained it. His glowing face, his air of well-being, his conversations with his schoolfellows bore witness to the change in him. He was found talking seriously with the very Christian teachers whom, a few days previously, he had been mocking, and consorting with some of the little Christian community in the bazaar, and his conversion became the subject of crude or angry talk throughout Rampur. Almost at once persecution broke out.

His family, finding that they could not persuade him to forego his new faith, joined with and finally led the boy's oppressors. His schoolfellows played tricks on him as Sundar had done to his teachers; his brother cursed him at home and outside, putting out false rumors that were difficult to counter; and in the streets people spat in the dust as he passed.

Open persecution ceased when Rahmat Ullah, the most violent of Sundar's enemies, died an agonizing death from cholera. Instead, it was turned upon the Christian community as a whole. Before long, the little group of Christians found the village shops closed against them, their houses damaged, and their possessions destroyed. In despair they escaped, slipping away, to find a home at a village called Ropur, where there was already a Christian pastor and a dispensary at work.

A schoolfellow whom Sundar had influenced provided a more frightening example of what he might expect if he continued as a Christian. This Sikh boy was withdrawn from school, forced to the lawcourts to bear witness against his teachers, and eventually poisoned so that he might no longer disgrace his family.

Sundar knew well enough that his father's love, now that it could command him no longer, was turning to desperate anger, and that if he persisted in calling himself a Christian he might well suffer the same fate as his friend. Sher Singh, however, found it easier to be kind when his son was out of sight, and allowed him to go, unmolested, to a Christian boys' boarding school in Ludhiana. From a distance, Sher Singh pleaded and commanded.

Indian boys celebrate their coming of age earlier than those in the West, and are considered adults when they are 16, but Sundar was not yet 15. He might declare himself a Christian, but unless his father agreed, he could not be baptized until he was of age. Was there no way of binding him to the family? If he were married, for instance . . . ? Sher Singh wrote to his son about marriage and, before he reached the end of his letter, brought up all the arguments he could command.

"My dear son, the light of my eyes, the comfort of my heart—may you live long. We are all well here and hope the same for you. .... I order you to get married immediately! ... Make haste and don't disappoint us. .... Does the Christian religion teach disobedience to parents?

".... You have gone mad! Just think for a moment. Who will take care of all our property? Do you want to blot out the family name? If you get engaged I will bequeath you all the sum of money now in the three banks (the interest of which amounts to three or four hundred rupees a month); otherwise you will lose what I have reserved for you.

".... It will be for you good if you come home at once. ....

".... I am not well. ...."

Sundar read the letter again, put it in his pocket, said a reluctant farewell to the headmaster and the matron, and returned to Rampur.

When he arrived he was greeted with evident relief and affection. His father put his arms about the boy's neck and led him indoors.

"My son!" There were tears in Sher Singh's eyes. "You have returned to do as I bid you!"

Sundar was silent for a moment. When he spoke, his words were like a dagger thrust. "No, Father. I cannot do as you bid me. I am the servant of the Lord Jesus. I have returned because the Christian boys at the school were not what I expected. Perhaps I am proud, but I just couldn't work with them or live with them. I must follow Jesus, but I must follow Him in my own way ... and I must follow Him here, in Rampur, not in Ludhiana, among boys who have never really known Him."

There followed another period of mingled persuasion and persecution, the latter growing more determined as the weeks passed."

His father bullied. His brother cursed. A favorite uncle took him to the cellar below his house and offered him all the wealth in his treasure chests. Sundar could give only one reply.

He gave it again a week or so later when his cousin, Spuran Singh, asked him to stay with him in the capital city of Nabha State. Here lived the maharaja. Spuran Singh held high office under the prince and had brought Sundar that the ruler of the state might make an appeal to him with all the official authority the Sikh so much respects.

Sundar was escorted to the audience chamber, the durbar hall, and found the prince seated on his throne, clad in ceremonial dress, his black eyes flashing like the jewels he wore in his ears and about his neck.

"Sundar Singh!" His voice was sharp with command. "Why do you bring dishonor on your race? You wear the bracelet of the Sikh; you wear your hair uncut, in the Sikh fashion; you bear the name of a Sikh. Why do you not behave like one? You are a 'Singh'—you know what that word means, the name your ancestors gave you?"

"Yes, my lord. It means 'lion.'"

"Why then do you, who bear the name of 'lion,' behave like a jackal, a low cur of the desert?"

Sundar made no answer. A little later he bade his cousin farewell and returned home. The words of the prince were ringing in his ears. "You have the name of a Sikh, the hair of a Sikh. ..." He must make some gesture that, once for all, would convince his family of his determination never to cease from his discipleship.

The first thing he did when he reached home was go to his own room and shear off the long hair that he wore after the fashion of his race and that had never been cut since he was a child. His father's wrath was dreadful to see. Not only had he defied the family, but he had brought shame on the race that had faced oppression and death rather than accept dishonor. This was an act of disobedience that could never be forgiven. In the presence of the family and of the servants, he was led to the door of the house as darkness fell. In the silent, sweet-smelling darkness Sher Singh spoke the words of outcasting!

"We reject you forever. In the name of the whole family, I declare you are no more worthy to be called our son. We shall have nothing to do with you. We shall forget you as if you had never been born. You will leave this house with nothing but the clothes you wear on your back. Now—*go!*"

With these words Sundar was driven from the village into the jungle beyond, where he spent the night under a tree, clutching his New Testament, his only possession, tightly in his hand. He was too happy at being called upon to suffer so openly for Jesus to notice the passing of the night, or even the pain that began to gnaw at his stomach.

When morning came he made for the railway line, intending to find his way once more to Ludhiana.

He had not been on the train more than half an hour or so when the pain grew worse. Suddenly he began to vomit, and blood oozed from his mouth. Then Sundar knew the truth. Not only had he been cast out, but before he left home poison had been put into the last meal he shared with his famlly. His death must wipe out the disgrace they felt so bitterly.

Fortunately, the boy was able to leave the train and crawl to Ropur, the village where the Rampur Christians had sought shelter. Here Mr. Uppal, the pastor, and a dispenser gave him treatment that almost miraculously saved his life, so that he was able to continue his journey a few weeks later to Ludhiana, where he stayed with two American missionaries until his 16th birthday drew near. Then he left them and went up to the quietness of the Simla Hills. He had been tempted to leave once or twice before, for his father could not forget him and had come to Ludhiana to plead with his son. The old man, broken, regretful, hobbling across the compound on his crutch, came nearer to persuading his son than ever before. Then, again, he had nearly left Ludhiana for the sake of the mission when the building was besieged by a gang of hooligans who threatened to destroy it if Sundar were kept there against his family's will.

Now he went to seek peace, to meditate in the towering pine forests that swept up to the gates of the Leper Hospital at Sabathu, where he made his temporary home. Through the trees he could see the sweltering plains of the Punjab. When he climbed up the steep hillside, he had glimpses of the eternal snows of the Himalayas, rose-pink in the sunrise, cutting off the closed land of Tibet beyond. As he wandered, looking, praying, trying not to plan too far ahead, one thought drummed in his mind over and over again.

Between those plains, that closed land, and these hills must lie my future.

At the beginning of September he climbed the hill paths through the forests that led to the town of Simla. He walked up the Mall, past government offices, private houses, and shops, and stood looking at the solid block of Christ Church, which dominated the little plateau in the center of this hill station. Running past it went the road that led across the hills to Tibet.

On September 3, 1905, he was 16.

On that day, his birthday, he was baptized as a Christian by Rev. J. Redman and Canon Chandu Lal.

Four weeks later his real lifework began.

5

1906-8

Sundar Dons the Yellow Robe

Whatever might lie in the future, the past was dead. Until the day he stood, quite alone, making his confession of faith before the altar of the Simla church, there had been the chance of going back. Now he was a baptized Christian, a member of a small and despised community, regarded as worse than dead by his family, and with few friends among the Christians themselves. Indeed, he owed more to the missionaries than he did to his own people, for while the missionaries regarded him as a triumph of the grace of God, the Indian Christians were inclined to think him proud, young, and overzealous. Within Christ Church, as he knelt for his baptism, his loneliness was something wonderful, a separation from the things of this world, an exaltation into the intimate presence of God. As he left the church behind and set off back to Sabathu, looking like any other Indian boy whom he passed on the cart track or the forest paths, his loneliness was of a different kind. No one could help him now. The struggle was his own; the decision must be his own; and there might be weeks or months of bitter mental strife before he could come back, clear-minded, into the everyday world.

The struggle must be his own! He trudged onward, his bare feet stabbed now and then by jungle thorns. The words

33

of his favorite psalm, which had been used at his baptism, sounded in his ears. He stood still. Apart from the tiny sounds of the forest, there was silence. The wind sighed in the fir trees and a tiny, chattering monkey dropped onto the path a few feet ahead. Sundar listened. Was that voice in his own heart, or speaking from the path beside him? "I am thy Shepherd. . . . I will lead thee! Thou shalt not want! Though thou walkest through the valley of the shadow of death thou shalt fear no evil . . . Goodness and mercy shall follow thee all the days of thy life."

Sundar turned, half expecting to see the speaker. The voice was real. The Speaker was real. And yet He was not there. But it was not the voice of Mr. Redman or Canon Chandu Lal. It was no memory. It was unlike any voice he had ever heard—except the voice that had once spoken to him in his own room in Rampur. Sundar knew that to the end of his life he would never be alone again.

His strange, mystic sense of God, breaking through the physical barriers of this world, would always endear him to the East and perplex the West. Indeed, only an unimpeachable sincerity of life could protect him against the results of his own mystical experiences, for pride comes easily to the popular saint in India.

A shaft of sunlight lit his face as he moved forward, and immediately afterward he was lost in the fantastic shadows of the trees and the undergrowth. He was lost to his friends for almost a month, fighting his spiritual battles in solitude, like the sadhu of the Rampur jungle.

During those weeks his thoughts often turned to the ancient hermit. He heard his mother's words: "It may be that one day you, too, will become a sadhu." Could anything be more satisfying than communing with God among these Himalayan forests? Was there any place for him in the Indian church? *He* was a village Indian; the church had lost its way and was too Western for him to fit into. Its existence and manners it owed to the West. Its hymns were translations, its services adaptations of those to be found in Britain or America. Its members, relying on the missions for their livelihood, imitated the missionaries' customs. They learned English, ate in Western ways, and dressed in Western clothes. Their intention had been to show the Hindus and Muslims round about them that they had forsaken the old gods, but the results were perilous. The Christian church had become the church of the West in India. To Sundar, even at this stage, it was clear that if the Indian church was to save its soul and, more important, to save the souls of the Indian people, it must present the Christian gospel in Indian terms. He must turn his back on a secure position within it. He must be true to his heritage—and his Savior.

What could be more Indian than the sadhu, the holy man lost in meditation and teaching little groups of those who sought him out in his retreat?

On October 3, exactly a month after his baptism, Sundar walked away from Sabathu. On his head was a yellow turban and about his body the yellow robe of the holy sadhu.

But he was a sadhu with a difference. It was the road, not solitude, that called him. "I am not worthy to follow in the footsteps of my Lord," he confessed, "but, like Him, I want no home, no possessions. Like Him, I will belong to the road, sharing the suffering of my people, eating with those who will give me shelter, and telling all men of the love of God."

It took a long time for his friends to accustom themselves to so apparently eccentric an idea. The average sadhu practiced self-discipline, even self-mutilation, in order to acquire merit; the Western preacher was firmly fastened down to a definite theology and a particular church organization. Sundar, however, combined the Indian ideal for self-denial, not for his own sake but for others, and the Western ideal of the preaching friar, and chose a vocation that was to revitalize the Indian church. His yellow robe won him admission everywhere, and though in many villages the fact that he was a Christian meant angry rejection, in others he was welcomed for that very reason. There was nothing of the graybearded saint about him—he was tall, well-built, and just 16 years old. Nor could he be confused with the half-mad, ash-smeared, tousle-haired, dirty mendicants who were so distressingly familiar. He was clean, vigorous, radiantly happy, and full of tales about the hills where he had been living.

He put his vocation to the test at once by returning to his own village of Rampur. Though he was still rejected by his own home, he was astonished to find a fascinated audience among the shopkeepers, the peasants, and the boys with whom, only a couple of years earlier, he had been at school. Even the *zenanas,* the women's quarters of the high-caste homes, were opened to him. He stayed with his Christian friends who had returned to the village from Ropur, where he had lain dying of poison.

They asked him what his plans were. "How long do you propose to remain a sadhu, friend Sundar?"

"I am wedded to these robes; and, God willing, I will never be divorced from them." It was the reply he would always give.

The unexpected welcome in Rampur was poor preparation for the months that followed. Brought up in luxury, and still scarcely toughened by his months in the hills, he set out on his first long winter tour. He began by wandering northward through the Punjab, over the Bannihal Pass above Jammu into Kashmir before it was blocked with snow, from Kashmir across the brigandlands of the northwest frontier to Baluchistan, and back into the fanatically Muslim country of Afghanistan. To attempt such a tour in winter was to ask for hardship, and Sundar suffered every bitter agony the climate and people could produce. His thin yellow robe was no protection against the frost and snow; he was unused to sleeping in the open, as he was often forced to do; his feet, without sandals to protect them, were cut and bruised, leaving a trail of bloody footprints along the village streets.

"The apostle of the bleeding feet" the Christian people of the north called him before many months had passed.

That first tour produced incidents that were to be matched again and again in his life. At Doiwalla, where they welcomed him for his yellow robes, he was thrust out into the driving rain as soon as he mentioned Jesus, forced to find shelter in a broken-down hut, where his only living company was a black cobra. Near Meerut a rough shepherd joined him, talked to him of spiritual matters that no shepherd might be expected to know, and disappeared out of sight, leaving Sundar to walk with bright eyes murmuring to himself the first line of his baptismal psalm. At Jallalabad the Muslims took him for a spy and would have killed him in his sleep if he had not been warned to escape; but when at last they found him in another village, his would-be murderers knelt before him to ask his forgiveness and plead with him to tell them his good news about Jesus.

In Simla, during the spring, he met a rich American, Samuel Stokes, a Quaker who wanted to give his life to the Indian people. In his company, instead of resting after his strenuous winter, Sundar undertook another long tour through the Kangra Valley, traveling at night, preaching and sleeping in the daytime, using a magic lantern in villages where it did seem indeed to be magic, going on and on until at last a vicious attack of malaria prostrated him and he and Stokes had to seek refuge in a kindly planter's house.

For Sundar that was the end of the journey; for the planter it was only the beginning of another one, for, impressed by the boy's character, he became a devout Christian. To Sundar, Indian and European, rich and poor, all needed the message of Christ.

For a while during the summer he worked with Stokes in the Leper Hospital at Sabathu, until plague stalked across the plains in the wake of dry, hot weather. Then he followed the American down to the dust again, from the coolness of the Himalayas, to work day and night, nursing as well as preaching to the plague victims in the Punjab villages and Lahore.

The next year, 1908, Samuel Stokes returned for a while to America. In the few months they were together he had taught Sundar much about the Franciscan ideal of the preaching friar and had confirmed his belief that in service and sadhuship was a joy to be found nowhere else.

6

1908

Across the Himalayas

Sundar was a born adventurer.

No one could talk long with him and retain the idea that he had adopted a sadhu's life as an escape from the demands of the world. Normally, he was shy with strangers and Westerners—he had suffered many rebuffs from them —but with his friends he spoke freely. They were always astonished by him. Within two years he had traveled all over north India, withstood heat, cold, plague, malaria, cholera, faced death a score of times, and learned more about nature, wild and human, than most professors understand in a lifetime. His friends were incredulous about some of his adventures, though they were always convinced of Sundar's personal honesty, wondering only whether his ecstatic experiences did not get mixed up with his everyday adventures. One thing they could never underestimate—the boy's utter consecration to God, his burning desire to be used for the spread of the gospel and the revival of the Indian church.

They discovered, too, that his adventurous spirit was already questing beyond the barrier of the Himalayas.

His retreat was always to the Simla Hills, the foothills of the Himalayas, where he had wandered before and after his baptism. Now, however, instead of staying at Sabathu, he climbed up to Simla. His tall, slim figure would be seen striding up the Mall, through the Lakri bazaar, past Kitch-

39

ener's home at Wildflower Hall, to Fagu, where the bare hillside meets the forests that stretch from Thandiani to Narkanda and Kotgarh.

It was at Narkanda, a tiny village 9,000 feet high, ringing all day with donkey bells as traders trudge along the hill paths, that Sundar came upon some farmers at work. Nandi was reaping in a field below the travelers' bungalow, with the valley hazily spread out below, when he looked up and saw the motionless figure of a holy man. Farmers have little time for holiness when they are gathering crops, and Nandi was irritated when the sadhu stepped down into the field and began to talk to them. It was bad enough when, for politeness' sake, they had to stop work and listen, but it was worse when they realized that this was neither Hindu nor Buddhist, but a masquerading Christian. Nandi's brother ordered the holy man away and flung a stone that cut deep above Sundar's eye. The reapers stood horrified, awaiting the curse of the sadhu. Incredulous, they heard him murmur, "Father, forgive him," and watched him anxiously as he moved away to bathe his face. In the middle of the afternoon Nandi's brother sank down in the field with a desperate headache. The villagers put it down to the magic of the sadhu and were amazed to see Sundar come quietly across the field, pick up the farmer's scythe, and continue his work.

That night Sundar spent at Nandi's house and talked for hours to a circle of deeply attentive villagers. There was a welcome for him whenever he passed that way again, and a certain superstitious dread when the next harvest came, for the field where Sundar had reaped yielded far greater crops than any of Nandi's fields had ever done before.

A mile or so beyond Narkanda, amid the giant pines of the primeval forest, the track divides, the main path going on to Bareri and a second leading down to Kotgarh. Here in Kotgarh, 7,000 feet up in the hills, 50 miles from Simla, amid the orchards and fields of Indian corn, Sundar had his retreat. It was not far from that of Mr. and Mrs. Beutel, the white-haired German missionaries who cared for the small dispensary and school nearby.

Sundar frequently climbed the path that continued past Kotgarh, through the forest glades and past open, cultivated land, until Rampur, the capital of Bashahar State, could be seen huddled in the burning heat of the Sutlej Valley. In Rampur, houses were built with curving Tibetan roofs. In the fields nearby were prayer flags. Long-haired yaks bore Tibetan merchandise, and traders with Mongoloid features bargained in the bazaars. In Rampur one could not forget that the dangerous track beyond, perilously following the high mountain ledges, led to Tibet, the closed land of central Asia. "Tibet is our own responsibility. The gospel has been brought to us, and we cannot keep it for ourselves. We must take it to Tibet, difficult and dangerous as the undertaking is." This was Sundar's challenge to the Indian church in later years. He himself faced the challenge 18 months after his baptism.

Missionaries had been trying every since the 14th century to establish the Christian church in Tibet. Every attempt had failed. The 6 million people who inhabited the Tibetan highlands lived in dirt, fear, and degradation. The rulers of the country were the lamas, the religious overlords who knew that travel, foreign traders from India or the West, education, and especially Christianity would destroy their power, based on the superstition and ignorance of the people. Nominally they were Buddhists, but many were little better than devil-worshipers, fanatical and cruel. Any outsider penetrated Tibet at his own risk, but to try to cross the Himalayan barrier to preach the Christian gospel in this closed land implied not the risk but the certainty of death.

Sundar took that risk not once but many times, year after year, facing, in addition to the hostility of lamas and people, the hundred various hazards of the snow-clad, precipitous Himalayas.

His first attempt, in the early summer of 1908, when he was 19 years old, led him only to Lesser Tibet, on the plateau far beyond Rampur and the Sutlej Valley. He was aided by two Moravian missionaries, Kunick and Marx, who gave him hospitality at Poo, a border town, taught him something of the Tibetan language, and lent him a young interpreter, Tarnyed Ali.

Sundar was appalled at the state of the people. Their airless homes, like their persons, were filthy. The Tibetans were horrified when they saw Sundar bathing in an icy stream and thrust him out of the village, for "holy men never wash." The only food he could obtain was parched barley, often so hard that even mules refused to touch it. Tibetan tea, mixed with salt and flavored with a ball of rancid butter, was hardly more pleasant. Prayer flags fluttered everywhere, and peasants carried prayer wheels with the mystic words, *"Om mane padme hum,"* inscribed on the paper within them. Sundar's open proclamation of Jesus infuriated the people and the lamas alike, and with his interpreter he tramped from village to village, homeless and rejected. The only kindly reception was at Tashigang, a little fortified town, where the lama, who ruled over a colony of 400 lesser priests, welcomed him and gave him liberty to preach in the monastery. After this, hostility increased still further, and when he turned back to get through the passes before snow closed them for the winter it seemed hardly worthwhile ever to think of returning.

Nevertheless he was hardly back in Kotgarh before he was planning to return the following year as soon as the passes opened. That first inhospitable journey was the first of a score between 1908 and 1929. There was never one without danger, and on most of them he faced death.

7

1909-11

Escape from Security

"I want to go to Palestine more than any other place in the world," Sundar confided to his friends. In 1908 he went to Bombay and was bitterly disappointed when the government refused to grant him a permit. Instead, he had to return to his north Indian villages. As he sat in the train he was meditating on the fact that Jesus was, like himself, an Easterner, and that the gospel had first been carried to India, according to tradition, not by Western missionaries but by a Syrian apostle.

There was a commotion when the Frontier Mail train stopped at a wayside station and, from the long third-class carriage where Sundar was sitting, a Brahmin priest was carried onto the platform. He had collapsed in the noisy, crowded, overheated carriage. Sundar watched the Anglo-Indian stationmaster running forward with a cup of water from the refreshment room and saw the fainting Brahmin wave it away in horror. He would not pollute his lips with a common cup even to save his life. Then a companion from the train appeared with the Brahmin's own brass bowl. The fainting man clutched it, drinking greedily. As the train moved on, with the sick man revived and safely back in his carriage, Sundar turned to those sitting near him.

"That is what I am always telling my Christian friends. We are offering Christianity in a Western cup and India rejects it. But when we offer the water of life in an Eastern bowl, then our people will recognize it and take it gladly."

Sundar found himself in the very center of the Indian church's most urgent problem. Christianity was regarded as a Western accretion to the religions of India, its main exponents were Western missionaries, and many of those who accepted it found security in church or government service. To him it seemed clear that if Christianity did not become an indigenous faith, expressed in Indian terms, it must fail. To one who valued his cultural heritage so much, it was incredible that Indian Christians should cut themselves off from it.

"If *that* is what you think—and you're probably right—then you have a duty to the Indian church as well as to the non-Christians outside," said one of his intimate missionary friends a few weeks later. "I know how much you love your sadhu's robe, and how valuable is your preaching in the villages. You *are* offering India the water of life in an Eastern bowl. But you must teach the church to offer it in that way too. If you have an experience of Christ to share with the Hindu and Muslim, then surely you should share it also with the halfhearted Christian in the church."

Under pressure from his friends, Sundar consented to spend a year or two at St. John's Divinity College in Lahore. From the beginning he felt restricted and unhappy. He sustained himself only with the thought that Bishop Lefroy of Lahore believed that if he were ordained he could give the church a vision that no one else at that time could pass on. Nevertheless, it needed all the bishop's tact and kindness to keep him at St. John's.

He had done very little regular study, though he was still young enough not to find it difficult. He listened to lectures on the Bible and the prayer book and found them unreal compared with his personal knowledge of Jesus and easy, natural meditation. He wrote essays on comparative religion and theology and found his mind wandering across the snow-bridges of the Himalayas.

He was not an easy companion. His fellow students regarded him as unique and eccentric, with his yellow robe and reserved nature, while he found them callow and noisy. With his rigid standards of behavior and devotion they seemed utterly worldly, and he saw little hope for the church when they became its ministers; from their point of view, he was pious and hypercritical. The differences of outlook and character between Sundar and his fellow students were too great at the time for them to understand one another. His very reputation outside the college put him at a disadvantage with the students.

This period came to an abrupt end when, one day, the ringleader of his tormentors came quietly upon him sitting under a tree in the college compound. He realized with a shock that Sundar was praying for him: "If I have done anything to hurt him or anger him that he treats me in this way, forgive me, O God, and show me my sin that I may overcome it." The listener moved forward broken by Sundar's anguished prayer, and touched the young sadhu on the shoulders. From that moment they were close friends. Teasing ceased. But Sundar was never really happy at St. John's.

The final shock came at the end of his college career. He had been granted a license to preach by the metropolitan of India and went to talk with the saintly Bishop Lefroy about his ordination. He spoke again of his ideals, of his hope to travel throughout India awakening the church.

"My dear Sundar, if you are ordained in our church you cannot wander all over the country. You will have one church, or perhaps a group of churches, to care for. You will certainly have to remain in the diocese where you are ordained. You cannot go and preach in Bombay or Nasik or Calcutta or Benares without the permission of the bishop there." He looked at Sundar's horrified face. "I thought you understood that," he went on.

"No; not *that!* And Tibet?"

"Tibet belongs to nobody, certainly—but you cannot leave your diocese for four or five months in the hot weather to lose yourself in Tibet."

Sundar was shocked, though he should have realized earlier what ordination would mean. He had assumed that he would be allowed to continue his normal vocation even if he were ordained. Bishop Lefroy was gentle and helpful, but he was not surprised when Sundar returned his license to preach within the diocese and made it plain that he could never accept ordination on such limiting terms.

From that time Sundar worked as a free agent, a typical sadhu, wandering wherever he would. His experience in college had given him a deeper sympathy with the minister who was bound to a local church, but it confirmed him in his belief that the Western organization of Christianity was completely unsuited to India. There was no division between himself and the organized church. Wherever he went he was normally received with gladness and fellowship, and 10 years later was welcomed throughout the world as one offering a unique contribution to the life of the church, but he chose to follow the vocation of the sadhu because in that way he could give most to the land he loved.

In particular, at this period he exerted great influence on the students of India. One of his greatest friends, Susil Rudra, was principal of St. Stephen's College, in Delhi, and the world-famous C. F. Andrews was on the staff. Sundar spent a good deal of time during the cold weather traveling and was often passing through Delhi. He made St. Stephen's his home. He was very little older than many of the students, for he was still under 25, and they thrilled to his tales of Tibet and the northwest frontier, as they did to his simple, practical conception of religion. His influence in this group was immense.

Many of the future leaders of the Christian community were students at St. Stephen's, and they loved to trek up to

Kotgarh on their vacations to stay with the young sadhu. From time to time Susil Rudra wrote to Sundar and gave him news. It was strange news from a group of students so wedded to the doctrine of secure respectability:

"Samuel has decided to give up his government career and enter the ministry of his church."

"Young Matthai scored a century on Saturday. He is still set on his social service job."

"Theofilus spent three whole nights sitting in the sweepers' quarters, nursing one of the sweepers who had contracted cholera—and you know what Theofilus used to think about the unclean, outcaste sweepers!"

"Amrit Singh came into Kotgarh yesterday carrying a hillman on his back. He had found him two miles out, lying in the forest, suffering from plague. As a physical feat it took some doing, but the courage of it far outweighs that!"

The names are altered, but the incidents, and many other like them, are true. The influence behind them was the young man in the yellow robe who was just starting off again from Kalka for his summer expedition to Tibet.

This time he proposed to go across the Kailas Hills.

8

1912

The Maharishi of Kailas

"I don't know how he thinks of it all. But he *must* make these things up. They simply *can't* be true!"

There were many people who said this about adventures Sundar recounted, such as the stories of the Maharishi, the Sannyasi Mission, and the escape from the well at Razar. It might be possible that some of the stories he told about himself were merely projections of his own imagination in a period of trance, or even of mountain sickness, for Sundar was a true mystic. Yet he spoke little about his less credible adventures, desiring to be heard for the sake of the gospel alone. Against the charge that he embroidered and exaggerated must be set the facts that he traveled constantly in remote and unsurveyed regions, and that other travelers occasionally produced evidence supporting Sundar's most fantastic experiences.

The year 1912, just after he had returned his preaching license to the metropolitan, produced two of his most amazing encounters.

He planned to enter Tibet that year by an unaccustomed route across the famous Kailas Range, to the north of Garhwal—a region known as the Mount Olympus of India, where the ancient Hindu gods lived and played. There is no lovelier spot in the world than the great Mansorowar Lake, high among the hilltops, with its wild swans and crumbling Buddhist temples. All is solitude. Across the plateau range nomadic robber bands, waiting to swoop on the pilgrims and the Tibetan caravans coming from the market town of Gianame. Here, too, it was said, were holy men who had left the world to engage in meditation and prayer. Sundar hoped to meet some of them as he crossed into Tibet.

The beauty of the scene stirred his soul, but, vigorous mountaineer though he was, the rigors of the climate and the road left him prostrate. At last, worn out with climbing, staggering over rocks and crags that he could not see because of snow blindness, he suddenly fell. How long he was unconscious he never knew, but when at last he opened his eyes he was horrified by the sight before him. He thought the creature with matted hair, wizened face, and a brown-furred body was a wild animal. Only when it spoke did he recognize that it was an incredibly old man. He was too sick with cold to move as the dreadful-looking creature came toward him, thrusting at him some green leaves with a motion that he should eat them. As he chewed them, hesitantly at first, the warm blood began to flood through his chilled body and he was able to sit up and look around him.

Suddenly the creature spoke, and Sundar was overwhelmed with astonishment.

"Let us pray together."

Sundar knelt by the side of the hermit and listened to a wonderful prayer that ended with the name of Jesus. Not only had Sundar stumbled by accident into the cave of one of the holy men he sought, but he had actually discovered a *Christian* hermit.

For many days Sundar remained here, entranced both by the recluse's life story and his ecstatic experiences. The visions the ascetic recounted, asserted Sundar, would have read like a new Book of Revelation. Many, indeed, he refused to repeat, so strange were they, but some he did retell were afterward published, without Sundar's permission.

Strange though they are, they bear a clear likeness to some of Sundar's own mystical writings.

The "great saint"—he was known to those who had heard the legends of his existence as the "Maharishi"—told Sundar that he had been living among the Kailas Ranges for almost three centuries. Born at the beginning of the 17th century in Alexandria, he had been brought up a strict Muslim. Seeking peace, he had entered a dervish monastery, but the more he read the Koran the less satisfied he was with Mohammed's religion. At last he sought out a saint who had come from India to preach in Egypt. This was Yernaus (the Arabic form of Hieronymus), the nephew of St. Francis Xavier, and through him he had been converted to Christianity. The very words that had challenged Sundar he himself had heard repeated: "Come unto me, all ye that labour and are heavy laden"; and, "God so loved the world, that he gave his only begotten Son." After accompanying his teacher on missionary journeys, he later parted from him to preach in the East. Overwhelmed with the sin and suffering of India, he had, almost 300 years ago, sought refuge in the Kailas Hills, where he had remained ever since, meditating and eating little but herbs.

As proof of his unbelievable story, he drew from a corner of the cave an ancient vellum roll of the Scriptures written in Greek uncial characters, which he asserted Francis Xavier himself had once possessed.

Such was the story young Sundar had to tell on his return from Tibet. There were many who pointed out that the Rishi's life story was not unlike Sundar's own, that the words he used were those that Sundar had heard before his conversion, that the visions and illustrations were such as Sundar himself used, and that the whole tale had the marks of an ecstatic experience. On two other occasions Sundar claimed to have revisited the Maharishi, but no one else had ever identified the hermit or the cave where he dwelt. On the other hand, an American engineer and a Christian preacher claimed to have met ancient hermits like him in the Kailas Mountains, while Tibetan traders say that the Maharishi himself has long been spoken of in their villages.

Less improbability is attached to the story of the Sannyasi Mission.

He had been preaching in Benares to the pilgrims who sought forgiveness by bathing in the sacred river, the Mother Ganges. At the pilgrim shrines he was always sure of interested, if sometimes violent, listeners. On this occasion some of his bearers assured him that while they themselves could not answer his arguments there was a *sannyasi,* a holy man like himself, farther up the riverbank who would confute all he said. To their chagrin, when they confronted the sannyasi with Sundar their own holy man put his fingers first in Sundar's mouth and then in his own, indicating that their words were, the same. Then they listened with bitter astonishment as the sannyasi began to proclaim Jesus to them, as Sundar had been doing an hour before.

This was Sundar's introduction to one of the strange underground Christian movements of modern India.

As he stayed that night in the sannyasi's hovel on the riverbank, he discovered that he was far from being the only Christian sadhu in India. Throughout the country there were holy men, secret followers of Jesus, whose traditions reached back for hundreds of years. They claimed that their order had been founded by St. Thomas himself in the first century, and that there are now somewhere between 20,000 and 40,000 members.

Later, Sundar attended their services and found them worshiping in Christian buildings that, from outside, looked exactly like Hindu shrines and temples. Here they observed the Christian rites of baptism and Holy Communion, though their worship took Eastern forms. Their hymns were Indian lyrics, and when they prayed they prostrated themselves on the ground before the holy place where, in a Hindu shrine, the idol would have been found.

When Sundar tried to persuade them that they should openly declare themselves as Christians, they assured him that they were doing a more effective work as secret disciples, accepted as ordinary sadhus, but drawing men's minds toward the true faith in readiness for the day when open discipleship became possible.

Others beside Sundar have met with the Sannyasi Mission. Carey himself, in the first days of Protestant missionary work in Bengal, is said to have encountered them. It seems doubtful whether they are really very strong either in Christian conviction or in numbers, but it is difficult in the light of Sundar's later experiences, especially in Garhwal and Nepal, to doubt their existence.

9

1912

Sundar Singh Is Dead!

Six of Sundar's friends received a telegram on the same day.
Each of their telegrams bore the same wording and had
been sent from the same place. Each was signed with the
single name "Smith":

"Sundar Singh sleeps in Jesus."

The words could only mean that Sundar Singh was
dead.

After his experience with the Maharishi and his dis-
covery of the secret Sannyasi Mission, Sundar had been ap-
proached by Canon Sandys of Calcutta, who wished to
know whether he would go to British Columbia. There was
a scheme to send an Indian Christian to minister to 4,000
Sikh lumbermen at work there. Who could be better than
Sundar Singh, himself a Sikh, who was used to the roughest
and most trying conditions? The Canadian government,
however, finally refused to grant an immigration permit,
and Sundar had once more to turn back to India.

As he traveled from Calcutta to Bombay, he thought of
the other time when he failed to go to Palestine, and when
he left Bombay for the north his mind was full of a desire
he had long cherished. At St. John's College at Lahore he
had read and reread Thomas à Kempis's *Imitation of Christ*. It
did not seem inappropriate to him that his whole life
should be such an imitation. The foxes and jackals had their

53

lairs, but he, like the Son of Man, had nowhere to lay his head. He deliberately refused to carry money, for Jesus had so commanded His apostles. He had taken Jesus at His word and could say that he did not love father or mother more than his Master. His rejections, his sufferings, his wanderings mirrored the ministry of Jesus in Palestine. His deepest desire was for companionship in the sufferings of Christ. So fully did this longing possess him that his intimate friends knew that he would joyously have accepted martyrdom. Some even found a deep sadness in him when he later passed the age of 33 and was compelled to live longer than the Master he loved.

When he neared Hardwar, a sacred Hindu city near Dehra Dun, the sadhu joined an Englishman who, like himself, was going north. The stranger described himself as a doctor, but since he told Sundar that he was on his way to join a Roman Catholic monastic order in the northwest, his doctorate may have had nothing to do with medicine. Some who met him later certainly regarded him as a priest.

As they walked, Sundar unfolded his plan.

He felt that, like his Master, he ought at the beginning of his ministry to have fasted. This omission he now desired to remedy, not in slavish imitation of the story of Jesus, but in order to quicken his spiritual awareness and strengthen his sense of oneness with God. His fellow traveler tried to dissuade him. It was evident that for years he had been overtaxing his strength and was in no physical condition to withstand 40 days and nights of fasting. Sundar refused to listen, and when they parted made his way into the thick jungle that stretches between Hardwar and Dehra Dun.

A little later the "doctor" handed in six telegrams to the stationmaster at a wayside halt and asked him to dispatch them.

They announced Sundar's death.

There was consternation among his friends. Obituaries appeared in the papers. Services were held in Simla and Calcutta. A fund was quickly started for some kind of memorial to him. India began to assess the greatness of the son she had lost. Letters and inquiries poured in by post, telegraph, and telephone, but there could be no satisfactory answer. All that could be said was that the message had been handed in to the stationmaster by "a black-robed gentleman." It was too early for Sundar to be in Tibet and, in any case, his friends always knew when he began his summer tour. Had he been alive he would surely have come forward and prevented both the anxiety of his friends and the spate of newspaper reports and articles.

Then suddenly news came from Dehra Dun.

Some peasants, making their way through the forest to cut bamboo, had come upon a man lying in a little clearing, apparently dying. Constructing a litter of bamboo poles and leaves, they had carried him to the little Christian settlement of Annfield, but no one there had recognized the emaciated figure until a New Testament with his name on the flyleaf was found in the pocket of his faded yellow robe.

Many days passed before he was sufficiently recovered to describe what had occurred. Bansi, the son of Pastor Dharamjit, listened eagerly and passed on his story.

The sadhu had found a convenient clearing and, since he knew that he would not be able to count the days, had gathered 40 stones, intending to drop one each morning. At first meditation had been easy, but as the days passed, weakness clouded his mind. Then, physical sensations growing less acute while spiritual perceptions quickened, a feeling of remarkable peace and happiness invaded him. Though his hearing was affected, his sight seemed to grow clearer. Animals came toward him and even smelled him, but not even a leopard that paused on the edge of the clearing did him any harm. He became too weak to move the stones by his side. Then, one day, there was darkness.

No one ever knew how long the fast had lasted, for Sundar could not remember and the peasants had not noticed any stones. Certainly it could not have been 40 days. Foreshortened though it was, however, Sundar always asserted that the complete isolation and absorption into the Spirit of God had cleared up many doubts and given him new power for the whole of his life.

He was still only 24 years old—young enough to have his head turned by the present concern for his welfare and the later adulation he was to receive through India and the West. That he never changed from the simple preaching friar, full of humility and wisdom, suggests that the fast may well have achieved some of the purpose Sundar had in mind.

He recovered his strength rapidly, for his was no ordinary constitution, and before March was finished was planning again for his annual trek into Tibet.

This year produced another of the extraordinary events that so puzzled his friends.

From the day he crossed the mountains there was trouble. Villagers refused him hospitality. He was nearly drowned in the swift-flowing, icy rivers. Food was scarce. He was stoned and ill-treated. Lamas and priests led the peasants in their persecution. It was becoming increasingly clear that to preach Jesus in Tibet might well mean death, and it is probably only because death had so few terrors for him that he so often escaped it.

The disastrous journey culminated in a town called Razar, a huddle of squalid hovels dominated by a high-walled, fortified monastery. Sundar began his preaching in the marketplace, sleeping at night in the common *serai*, the unsheltered compound where traders and beasts herded together for warmth. News of his preaching at first drew interested crowds, but when an account of it was taken to the chief lama, interest changed to fear and fury.

One morning the guard from the monastery came upon them, seized the sadhu, and dragged him away to a brief trial. Gazing at the vindictive face of the Grand Lama, who sat in the wide hall surrounded by superstitious priests and overlooked by the devilmasks on the walls, Sundar knew the trial could have but one end. Cruelty is a mark of the Tibetan, at any rate under stress of fear, and their forms of execution well illustrate the spirit of their religion. The felon may either be sewn inside a wet yak skin that is left in the heat of the sun to dry and shrink until at last the man within is crushed slowly and agonizingly to death, or he may be thrown into a deep, dry well, on top of the corpses cast there before him, to die of starvation and disease.

Sundar found himself dragged to the well. The top was lifted and the violent, swearing people crowded round him, beating and thrashing him until at last a blow sent him headlong into the pit. As he lay, stunned, he heard the lid being secured and locked. The stench was sickening, for the ghastly place contained the bones and putrefying remains of many others who had died in the same way. He prayed, hopelessly, for deliverance.

How deliverance could come he had no idea. One arm was fractured. There was no means of climbing to the top. And even if he could have done so he knew that he could not get out, for the Grand Lama himself had removed the key of the well from his own girdle, and by this time it would be back on the jangling key ring under his robes.

Hours passed, and turned into days. Three days and nights passed, though in the fetid, unbearable air there was no difference between darkness and light. Suddenly he heard a sound at the top of the well. A key turned in the lock and the lid opened, creaking on its rusted hinge. A moment later a rope touched his face. At the end was a loop. He thrust his leg into the loop, grasped the rope with his good arm, and felt himself being slowly drawn upward. At the top he collapsed on the ground, filling his lungs with the fresh air of the night. When he looked around, his deliverer had disappeared.

The sadhu crawled slowly and painfully to the serai and spent the remainder of the night in snatches of sleep. When dawn broke he bathed, rid himself of the smell of death that clung to his yellow robe—and returned to the marketplace to preach.

An hour later the small marketplace was invaded by furious monks who seized him once more and pushed him through the bewildered crowds to the lamasery. Sundar stood again in the cold shadow of the hall, while the Grand Lama questioned him over and over again. Who had helped him escape? Was it a man or a woman? How had that one gotten the key? That, of course, was the central question: How had he gotten it and where was it now? There was only one key to the well and that should be in the lama's possession. The lama pulled aside his robes, stood up, and drew the bunch of keys from the chain at his waist.

"There is but one key to the well. It should be here. Who stole it to set you free? How . . . ?" The lama's Mongoloid features suddenly became inscrutable. He turned, furious and inwardly afraid, to the waiting monks. "Take this man away . . . away from the town . . . . Set him free . . . and never let him set foot again in Razar!"

The key of the well was on his own ring.

10

Buddhist Strongholds

Tibet is not the only land where Christian preaching is prohibited or dangerous. Sundar Singh, the adventurer, sought them all out. The report of an inhospitable tribe, a guarded frontier, or a country where Christ was not preached presented a challenge that could not be evaded. He was certain that God himself sent him to these inaccessible places, where few other Christian preachers could penetrate, and that God would care for him. This, he realized, meant no more than that God would give him courage, endurance, and peace of mind; it was no guarantee that he would be kept out of danger or even from death.

"Jesus told us," he said, "that the disciple is not above his Lord, nor he that is sent greater than Him that sent him. When we have left this life we shall not have a second chance of bearing the cross for Christ. We must therefore bear it all the more gladly now"

He had faced death too often to be afraid of it. It had stalked his footsteps through the jungles, in caves and deserted huts as he kept company with wild animals; it had threatened him in the snows and avalanches of the Himalayas; it had almost held him in Tibet. He said calmly that he would never fear it when it came.

"It is easy to die for Christ; it is *living* for Him that is so difficult," he told his friends.

As a matter of fact, death would not take him easily, at this period of his life, unless it took him unaware. He was over 6 feet tall, with splendid physique. His constant wanderings in every kind of weather had toughened his body, and the light in his deep-set, luminous, brown eyes came from an unquenchable fiery spirit within. He relied little on ordinary medicines or food, for he had long learned the secrets of the forests from those who lived in them, and cared nothing for luxury. His powers of endurance were tremendous, and he was driven by such a passion for his Lord's service that it was difficult to imagine him as anything else than intensely alive. Yet there was no boisterousness, no bravado about him; his courage and strength were seen in the serenity and poise of his bearing.

His peacefulness, his sense of fun, and especially his keen sense of the ridiculous, his quick response to need in those about him, his moods of withdrawal, and his penetrating use of illustrations taken from nature and from everyday life—all led men to say the same thing: "The sadhu is more like Jesus than anyone we have ever known." They quickly discovered that the secret that lay behind these qualities was something he also shared with Jesus. Like his Master, he knew the value, the compelling necessity, of quietness and meditation.

From Kotgarh he would retire to the hills and be lost for a few days. When staying with friends in busier places, he would slip away for a while, so quietly that none noticed his going. He seldom spent whole days in meditation, but his life as a wanderer, while not permitting regular habits, did give him opportunities for meditation as he walked alone.

His usual practice was to rise very early and begin the day by reading a chapter of the Bible.

Sundar seldom talked publicly of his devotional life, though his addresses were the product of much meditation and prayer. Now and again he opened his heart to his friends, however.

"Rising early, I begin by reading a chapter of the Bible. I make a mental note of the verses that seem suggestive," he told his friends who asked about his methods of meditation. "Then, when I have quietly read the whole chapter, I return to each of these verses and meditate on them, one at a time. After I have exhausted all that God can say to me through those verses at that time, I spend a quarter of an hour 'collecting myself' for prayer.

"I have no special posture for prayer. I may sit, or kneel, or stand. I use no words. I think only of those things that I have been reading, of the things I have been doing or intend to do, of the people I know, of myself, and of Jesus—such thought *is* prayer. And, in such prayer, *God* speaks, not man."

Between India and Tibet, among the towering peaks of the Himalayas, stretching for hundreds of miles from the Simla Hills to Assam, lie the hills and valleys of Garhwal, Bhutan, Nepal, and Sikkim. Within these hardly accessible territories lies some of the most magnificent scenery of the world. Fertile valleys twist below the forested hillsides, and above them tower the highest peaks of the world's highest ranges. Through these forests, and along the shoulders of the eternally snow-clad hills, narrow dangerous paths lead into Tibet. The sadhu used these tracks as alternative routes to that leading from Kotgarh, for he had become a well-known figure on the frontiers and there were many in Tibet who would have kept him permanently out of the country if they could. Both on his way to Tibet and on special tours he preached throughout these Buddhist strongholds.

Many stories could be told of these death-defying journeys.

At Kantzi, preaching in the marketplace, the sadhu was assailed by an angry crowd who beat him into unconsciousness. They picked up his limp body and began to wrap a blanket around it. The market grew fuller and fuller of shouting people, all trying to get a sight of the yellow-robed holy man who had penetrated the country and then had begun to preach an alien gospel. The shaven, thin-lipped priests looked on from the gateways or the roofs of their temples. At last the victim was rolled in the blanket, with only his head and feet to be seen. His turban fell off as they began to drag him out of the town.

There were many hands to pull the body into the forest, and scores of the short, squat Mongolian people stood watching as the executioners bent over the sadhu. There would be no way of escape. The blanket, tightly reroped about him, would be his shroud. The crowd wished they could see the leeches, the scorpions, the snakes crawling over the tortured body, getting between the blanket and the flesh to suck his blood and sting him to death. There might even be a prowling leopard or two before the night was out. . . .

Sundar drifted back to consciousness and hardly realized where he lay. His wounds hurt; his mouth was dry. He tried to stretch his limbs and found they would not move. High above him in the branches of the tree he saw bunches of luscious fruit hanging, ready for plucking. A sudden pain shot through his leg as a scorpion crawled onto his ankle. Not far away he heard the snarl of a mountain leopard. He saw again in his mind the angry, twisted faces of the crowd, the more bitter because of his yellow robe and his Christian preaching. There would be no help from people such as those, or from the priest who had accompanied them into the forest. He slipped back into unconsciousness.

When he wakened again it was because his face was being bathed. He stretched his arms—and found them free. The fruit that had hung on the tree seemed miraculously to have fallen into his very hands. His wounds were already bound up. Far away he heard the night cry of the prowling leopard, and everywhere about him the stirring of the forest. It was too dark to see the two men who stood by him. They were shadows, no more—and when they had led him beyond the jungle to safety he thought of them as angels. Indeed, he often referred to them in that way, for they seemed to have been sent by God, and they had certainly wrought a mighty deliverance for him.

But he knew who they were, for they had whispered in his ear before they left him: "We are secret disciples—members of the Sannyasi Mission."

At Srinagar in Garhwal a holy pundit called to confute the sadhu's teaching by a group of hotheaded, youthful persecutors turned out to be a member of this same group who declared himself ready to stand by Sundar Singh's side and proclaim the same gospel with him to all who would listen.

"There are many of us, you know, *Sadhuji*," he confided. "Secret believers: members of the Sannyasi Mission that you first met in Benares—preparing the way of the Lord."

They talked, to each other and to all who would listen, far into the moonlit night.

The Sannyasi Mission came to Sundar's rescue again in Nepal, the Gurkha kingdom where Buddhism holds undisputed sway and where the hills and valleys are studded with temples, some sacred to pure worship and some reputed to practice devil worship as degraded as anything in Tibet.

Everest and Kanchinjunga tower into the sky above the little town of Ghum. Here Sundar left his Tibetan companion Tharchin while he himself made his way to the forbidden village of Ilom.

The days that followed his arrival there were crowded with such suffering as even he had seldom known. He was first of all arrested and flung into prison, but that very experience seemed to fill him with joy—joy that he might suffer for Jesus' sake. In his Urdu New Testament he wrote: "Christ's presence has turned my prison into a blessed heaven. What will it be like in heaven itself?" So exultant was he that he could not help singing all night and preaching from the tiny window of his vermin-infested cell throughout the day. Crowds, reluctant to listen in the open marketplace, hung on his words when they came from his prison.

Guards, hastily summoned by the infuriated magistrates, suddenly entered the little cell and dragged the sadhu into the courtyard. He was flung down onto some rough boards, and found his feet fastened to them as Western prisoners used to be fixed in the stocks. Then his arms were stretched above his head and his hands fastened in the same way. One of the guards opened the prison gate and flung the wooden frame, with the sadhu stretched upon it, into the marketplace. By the shops, at the side, there was some shelter, but the stocks were thrown down in the dust in the center of the square, where the sun burned into the hot ground all day long.

The crowds milled about the half-conscious figure fastened to the boards, shouting furiously. They were silenced as Sundar once more began to sing what the people now recognized as a hymn of praise to Jesus.

With sadistic fury, priests and prison guards returned to drop scores of leeches on the prostrate captive. The people watched silently as the small, wormlike creatures crawled over the sadhu's naked form, sucking his blood and nibbling their way below the skin into his quivering flesh. Legs, arms, and body were soon everywhere broken by wounds, swelling and bleeding in the sun.

Sundar never ceased singing' or preaching the joys of following Jesus. The crowd listened incredulously.

He was almost unconscious when he was dragged out into the jungle beyond the town and flung down on a rubbish heap to die.

That night, from half a dozen houses, like shadows flitting in the moonlight, came men and women to succor him, to free him from his stocks, to dress his wounds, and to lead him to a place of safety. Once more, as Sundar told Tharchin when he at last staggered into Ghum, his rescuers were members of that underground Christian movement, the Sannyasi Mission.

me Danger

who listened. "You can't
...ines things!"

Because his own experience of life was so much wider, his traveling so much less conventional, than that of his hearers, there were always some who gaped at him and then dismissed him as a man who "imagined things." Not a few of the most incredible tales are told by others than himself, however, or are supported by unimpeachable witnesses.

There was the occasion, for instance, when the sadhu was traveling north from Bombay by train. A sharp-eyed little man got into the carriage, bearing with him an atmosphere of evil. Before long, he told his anxious fellow travelers that he was a sorcerer and, when one of the travelers scoffed at the idea, offered to prove his own words. Before the doubter had time to object he was hypnotized.

Sundar broke into the sorcerer's proceedings with a few words that drew the attention of the whole carriage. The man cast his evil eye on the sadhu. Sundar bowed his head and prayed. For half an hour the sorcerer mumbled, turned his charms, and cast his spells. Then he suddenly announced that the holy man had a book in his pocket that was preventing the spell from working. Sundar drew out a copy of St. John's Gospel and laid it on the seat. After another trial the wizard, who had had no previous knowledge of the sadhu, stated that there was a single page of the same book on the sadhu's person. Sundar had indeed picked up a page of the New Testament that had been lying on the floor, rather than leave it there to be trampled underfoot. He laid that on top of the Gospel, and finally at the sorcerer's request drew off his yellow habit, but without proving a happier subject for the hypnotist's powers.

When the sorcerer gave up, Sundar began. He spoke of the power that was greater than the power of evil, of the power that lay in this discarded Book. Just so did he find his opportunities of proclaiming the gospel.

His power over animals was as great as that over men. His friends, who had seen something of this uncanny control over jungle animals, found no difficulty in believing that they never harmed him.

He was once staying with a friend in the Simla Hills. After supper they were sitting on the veranda and the sadhu moved quietly away as conversation lapsed, slipping through the bushes and across the lawn toward the forest trees which bounded the garden. He stood there, gazing across the valley at the tiny lights of distant villages. Suddenly the man on the veranda rose to his feet and stood tense, terrified by what he saw. Creeping slowly out of the trees at the side of the garden came a leopard, its tail outstretched, its belly almost touching the ground. It paused, gazed at the motionless sadhu, then moved deliberately toward him. The watcher dared not shout, for fear he would cause the animal to spring, and yet he did not know how to keep silent. Quietly the sadhu turned, saw the animal, and stretched out his hand toward it. The leopard rose, moved forward, and stood by the almost motionless Sundar, who stroked its sleek head as he would have done that of a pet animal. The watcher slowly relaxed. There was no longer any need for fear; there had never been such a need. The leopard stood, swaying slightly, now and again lifting its head to the speechless man, until the sadhu had finished his meditation. As Sundar turned to the house, the leopard's long, lovely, powerful form was lost to sight among the trees.

About such adventures as those there could be no question. Independent witnesses saw them, though Sundar himself never spoke of them. To him, they were all part of the everyday happenings inevitable to such a man as himself. To what did this young man owe his safety, his immunity from danger, his authority over wicked men and wild beasts? Some observers would have spoken of calmness, confidence, remoteness; others of an acquaintance with nature deepened into intimacy among the hills and the forests; yet others of an impenetrable aura of sanctity shared with holy men of Hinduism and Islam. Sundar himself had no hesitation in claiming that God protected and empowered those who trusted in Him.

Sundar trusted God for food, for money, for protection, for guidance. Tour after tour showed that God would prevent neither his entering into temptation nor his being hard pressed by suffering and persecution. His faith was no insurance against a much harder lot than that of other men. Yet he could always say that God kept His promises and delivered him from evil. In that faith he could—and did—face anything.

There were those who have asserted he possessed an uncanny power of rendering impotent the evil of others, and there were many other occasions when the power of God seemed manifest.

None of the opportunities passed, however, without Sundar seizing them as moments for preaching the gospel. He spoke simply, forcefully, to those with whom he dealt. They could understand what he said, and his illustrations were taken, as he said, from the two books he knew best—nature and the Bible.

"In every home there are spiders. Many of us," warned the sadhu, "trying to get rid of sin, are like housewives who destroy the spiders' webs without destroying the spiders."

Passing through a Himalayan region, Sundar came to a place where grew some herbs that sent the traveler to sleep as he breathed. A friend gave him another herb to smell as he passed, and its scent more than nullified the effect of the poison. So it is, he declared, with prayer and temptation.

Such was his method of talking to all who would hear, and throughout India were hundreds whom he had met on the road, in the marketplace, and on the train and whom he had introduced in this way to Christ.

"A Christian," he declared, "is a man who has fallen in love with Christ."

12
1918-19

The Power and the Glory

By the beginning of 1918 Sundar Singh was one of the most notable religious figures in India. His fame had carried not only to Christians but to Hindus and Muslims, Sikhs, and Parsees as well. His swinging gait, his honest eyes, his cleanliness, all distinguished him even to the casual observer from the cringing, deranged, and mendacious majority of "holy men." The accounts of his intrepid adventuring in the forbidden territories fascinated those who had not heard or read a word of his religious teaching. Above all, to the sincere religious seekers of India his simple, forthright, practical messages about God and men marked him out to be reverenced and followed.

Before he was out of his 20s, his reputation had spread to every district of the Indian subcontinent. When it was known that he would speak in any town, earnest as well as curious people thronged its streets and crowded its *dharmsalas,* or lodging places. When he came home to the Simla Hills from his Tibetan tours, piles of letters awaited his attention. Many were from friends or casual acquaintances, but more and more came from strangers persuading him to extend his preaching tours to their own towns.

The sadhu conferred with his close friends in Simla and Delhi. It was becoming evident that he could not continually refuse these requests. He possessed a message that the whole of India ought to hear. Already those who had come in contact with him in the north were beginning to play a very different and more effective part in the life of the Christian church than they had at one time intended or desired. Students from St. Stephen's College in Delhi, where he used to sit 10 years earlier talking in the common room or in Susil Rudra's house, were leading the Indian church along the road that Sundar had dreamed about—away from too clinging a dependence on the Western missionary toward an indigenous expression of Christian faith and worship.

It had now been amply proved that the unusual young man was right who had exchanged the security of a college and a parish for the freedom and jeopardy of a sadhu's life. Now, however, friends began to shake their heads in mistrust of his judgment, asking if a new and greater danger were not at hand. For 10 years, since he had made his first journey to Tibet, Sundar's personal fame had been spreading. Was it not now possible that he would suffer the same fate as other young men who had trodden the flowery path—success, flattery, adulation, then pride, and finally disaster?

Those who were intimate with him did not fear the onslaught of such a temptation. They knew him as a simple Christian, constantly turning away from men to Jesus, humbled afresh by his Savior's love. Indeed, the world seemed to mean less and less to him. He lived in a strange inner universe of spirit, and it was difficult at times to decide to which order the experiences he described belonged. His few writings were as profound as anything the medieval mystics had left. His sense of the intimate presence of God could be almost frightening, and the reality of the spirit world made him intensely angry with the materialism of many to whom he preached.

"He will never be tempted by pride," his friends assured each other.

They were wrong.

At the beginning of 1918 the sadhu went south. His first large meetings were held in Madras, and at once his limitation was apparent. His natural tongue was Hindustani, the common language of the north. He was at home, too, among many of the northern Indian dialects and languages and had learned English well enough for conversational purposes; but here in the south he was faced with a congregation whose main speech was Tamil. The problem was solved by a Hindu gentleman who offered to translate his address. Even in its probably inadequate translation, his words deeply moved his audience.

From Madras he passed on from town to town, his fame preceding him and the congregations growing. Arcot, Travancore, Trivandrum—through all the centers of Christian activity and many where ancient Hinduism was entrenched he moved in triumph. In the mornings he spoke with missionaries, preachers, teachers, and leaders where he could do so. He addressed Bible meetings, testimony meetings, meetings for worship, and meetings for witness. People gathered by the great tanks, under the palmyra trees by the roadsides, in the square before the sacred temples, in the wide, dry beds of the rivers. Sometimes there were 500, sometimes 10,000 listeners. Every meeting was followed by questions, discussion, throngs of people who desired personal interviews about personal and private problems. In each town the Christian community was stirred to revival and hundreds of non-Christians showed themselves seekers after the truth.

The sadhu had never been used to such a succession of public meetings. The sense of being organized wherever he went, of having all his plans made by others, and above all of having hardly any time for Bible reading and meditation began to oppress him. He almost refused when appeals were made that he should not neglect Ceylon on this tour.

In this island of priceless beauty, with its luxurious vegetation, its long sands and sweeping breakers, its gaily

71

dressed throngs, its eager students, its treasured remains of primitive Buddhism, a new sense of power came to the sadhu. He was asked to visit a boy named Williams who was in the hospital. He did so, praying by his bedside for the lad's recovery. The following morning, to the amazement of the hospital staff and the excitement of the Christian community, young Williams rose from his bed, completely well. The news flew round the town, round the island, and back to India.

The sadhu had the gift of healing.

Sundar had long been aware of this latent power; now, in anguished determination, he refused the appeals of those who sought him out that they and their loved ones might be healed. He might have the gift, but he must not use it. Were he to do so, he would be pressed in upon from every town and village in the land by those who desired healing, but who would not stay to thank the Savior whose agent he was, not even to hear the message he had to proclaim. They would come for what they could get. His healing would halt his message rather than enforce it. Sundar, as he had so often done, fought over the very battleground in which Jesus had striven so long before.

From Ceylon he returned for rest and peace to Bengal, where he stayed at the home of the great Indian poet Rabindranath Tagore, himself a friend of Sundar's greatly beloved missionary friend, C. F. Andrews.

Here was another example of what was now becoming so plain to the sadhu. Hindu, Buddhist, Sikh, Muslim, Christian—they would all listen gladly to the Christian gospel proclaimed in an Indian setting by an Indian who interpreted it in the traditional Indian terms. The rest of India did not follow the example of the animistic, superstitious Buddhist lands of the closed far north. There was no persecution, only deep respect wherever he went.

In the spring of 1919 the sadhu came down from his Tibetan fastnesses, where he had once more been face-to-face with death, to engage in a more extended series of tours. Failing to reach British Columbia or Palestine, he now went east to Burma. The great service in Rangoon Cathedral was the prelude to a victorious preaching tour that led him through Burma, Malaya, Panang, Singapore, on to China, and finally to Japan. Wherever he went his yellow robe, less familiar than in India, his face, and his commanding presence marked him out for distinction.

The difficulty of language was overcome in Singapore. In Penang he spoke his native tongue in a Sikh temple, and later addressed a meeting in the Empire Theatre, under the chairmanship of the superintendent of police, where his Hindustani speech was translated into English, Tamil, Malay, and Chinese. In Singapore, to his consternation, there was no one at his meeting able to translate. Hesitantly, after an urgent prayer, he began to speak—for the first time publicly—in English. From that time it was his normal language for addressing meetings other than in India.

His friends were becoming perturbed by this universal acclamation. To many in the East he looked and spoke like Jesus himself. It had been easy enough to speak of his essential humility before he set out for south India. But was there not now more than a slight danger that he would be spoiled by the worship of the crowds?

They had been wrong in their assumption that the sadhu's humility made him immune from the temptation to pride.

They were mistaken when they feared, overlate, that he might become its victim.

The sadhu had already fought out his battle in the lonely southern jungle country. It was some time afterward that he told them the story, in his own mysterious way.

He had sought solitude, he confided, and was engaged in meditation when a most noble person, looking like a priest, discovered him and began to speak to him. The sadhu, the visitor declared, was the man all India was looking for. He had proved that he could draw to himself men of every faith. He showed that there was a measure of truth in every religion. He was the first to discover that many roads led home to God. The Emperor Akbar had built a temple of all religions 400 years earlier, and the founder of Sundar's own religion, Guru Nanak, of the Sikhs, had found truth among Hindus and Muslims. *Now* was the time for another prophet, a guru who would bring all India to his feet. There were errors to be purged from all religions, but there was truth to be discovered too. What was needed was a teacher who could unite the best, discarding the unworthy. Jesus, in the new religion, would be the greatest Revelation of God the world had known, though Hinduism, Islam, and Buddhism would not be discredited ... and the sadhu, Sundar Singh, would be His prophet. He would go down in history as a prophet greater than Guru Nanak, greater than Mohammed, greater than ...

Sundar looked at the face of the noble person before him, saw the glittering mockery in his eyes, and knew him for the tempter, the evil one.

In that moment he was saved from disaster.

Those who listened wondered if the "noble person" had ever existed as a human being. But they knew the sadhu, in a mystical experience, had fought a desperate battle with himself, with his pride—and had won.

13

1919

Beyond the
Forbidden Door

"When do you expect to return, *Sadhuji?*"

Whenever he set off for Tibet his friends would ask the same question. The answer, too, was the same. Sundar would point out the arrangements he had made for his absence. Neither bank accounts—a fund collected for his Tibetan tours was lodged at the Alliance Bank in Simla—nor correspondence could be left to look after themselves, and trusted acquaintances took care of them for the wanderer. He would plan to return around a certain date toward the end of the hot weather. Then after summing up his arrangements in a thoroughly practical tone, the old faraway look would steal into his eyes. In a low, deliberate voice he would give his answer to the question of his return.

"I never expect to return from Tibet."

At no time would he have grieved about dying. The old Sikh ideal of martyrdom for the faith had been transmuted by the fact of the cross, which he expected to bear throughout his life, and on which he would have welcomed death when the end came. There was only one very human sadness that weighed with him. He would have loved a complete reconciliation with his father.

Sher Singh was still alive, a vigorous old man, in Rampur. Sundar visited the village now and then, finding that the people, and even his own household that had rejected him, had a regard for holiness and sadhuhood that overcame their hostility to his Christianity. If not welcomed, he was at least tolerated, and his fellow villagers were proud of the honor he had brought to Rampur; but the old barrier stood firmly between Sher Singh, the Sikh, and his yellow-robed son.

Sundar climbed toward the Himalayan peaks year after year, wondering if he would return again before the snows fell, and hoping for another opportunity of fellowship with his unbending old father.

The rift between them, and the possibility of its being continued to the death, was emphasized when Sundar brought back to the Punjab the story of Kartar Singh and his martyrdom.

Sundar, coming to the Tibetan town of Tsingham, met a man for whom the people had a superstitious reverence, one of the few who could preach about Jesus in this anti-Christian land without fear of reprisal.

This preacher had once been chief secretary to the lama of the town but, owing to the witness of a Christian missionary, had declared himself a follower of Christ. His first confession of faith was made to his own master, the fanatical, ignorant Buddhist lama. Within a few days he was sentenced, before the walls of the lamasery, to a pitiless death. Sewn into a wet yak skin and flung into the scorching sunshine, he was left to be crushed to death as the skin contracted. When he did not die quickly enough, red-hot skewers were thrust through the skin into his body and he was later withdrawn from the skin and dragged through the streets to the refuse heaps outside. Excruciating tortures were inflicted on him, and when he was finally dropped onto the dunghills, his breathless body fell awkwardly and awry. As the crowds left, the vultures began to gather.

The mutilated victim was not dead, though after this treatment he should have died of exposure; or of septic poisoning or starvation in the days that followed. Instead, he crawled back from the doors of death, and returned constantly to the village to preach.

When Sundar asked this astonishing man what had won him for Christ, the preacher's reply was that it was the witness of another martyr, done to death in this very same town and in an identical fashion. Within an hour or so of the end the dying man asked a moment's freedom for his right hand. With excruciating pain, he rolled toward a little Book that the crowd had left lying by his side. It was his New Testament. On the flyleaf, with writing material given to him by an onlooker, the martyr had written his last message!

"The life He gave to me was what I gave to Him."

The sadhu discovered that this young missionary, whose witness had had such remarkable results, was an Indian, a Sikh like himself from the Punjab, by name Kartar Singh. He, too, had been brought up in a home of luxury, had been made an outcaste by an enraged family, and had finally penetrated the Himalayas to preach to the devil-dreading Tibetans.

Sundar returned to the Punjab with the story of Kartar Singh's martyrdom and sought out the young hero's father. He had been without news of his son for years, and as Sundar told him of the boy's courage and the effect of his life and death, the old man's heart was broken.

He stretched out his gnarled hand and clutched at the sadhu's yellow robe. His fingers touched the sharp outline of the New Testament that Sundar always carried. His eyes filled with tears. "I believe in Jesus too," he whispered, choking over the words.

Sundar went out of the great house, and trudged slowly across the desert, his bare feet stirring a cloud of dust among the cactus plants. In such a house did his own father live. Such a proud Sikh was his father. If he could only hear *him* speak such words. . . .

Not only was Tibet inhospitable, fiercely antagonistic, when the traveler had penetrated its mountainous frontiers, but it made great efforts to keep would-be visitors out of its territory.

By the time he was 30 years old, in 1919, Sundar had been a dozen times or more in the country. Lama had passed on to lama the tale of his preaching tours and their results. The authority of the lama and the priest was challenged wherever Sundar stayed. He appeared impervious to hints, indifferent to threats, and immune from death. Word was passed along to the frontier posts that he must not be allowed to enter the country. The Tibetan government made it clear to British officials that he was an unwelcome immigrant and must be stopped.

His main route was from Simla through Kotgarh, but officials sometimes refused to allow him to use this road into Lesser Tibet. Another time, having gone beyond the frontier posts, he was turned back at Poo, where the Moravian missionaries had given him his first welcome 10 years earlier. Again, using alternative tracks from Garhwal and Nepal, British government officers refused to permit him to go farther than Gangtok and asked him to leave the country. Year by year he chose alternative routes in and out: from Simla, from the hills beyond Lucknow and Bareilly, through Almora, by Pitharagarh on the Nepal border, from Dangoli, across the dangerous Niti Pass beyond Badrinath, near Mansorowar Lake, where live the Maharishi of Kailas—as each was tried the Tibetan authorities extended their attempt to keep him out. Yet never a year went by without his making his way into the country for his summer preaching tour.

Man-made restrictions were not the most difficult to overcome. Even in the summer the passes were dangerous. Yaks, ponies, and hillmen fell to their deaths down the chasms and precipices that scarred the mountain tracks. Sudden snowstorms, coming far out of season, made the roads impassable. The cold, even in the height of summer, was always intense above the eternal snow line, yet Sundar never wore sandals and had little but his yellow cotton robe to wrap around him for protection. He was a man of immense physical courage, sustained by inexhaustible spiritual reserves.

On one occasion, after he had seen the frozen corpses of travelers who had died in the snow, a driving snowstorm overtook him and his Tibetan companion. At first it blinded them and forced them to their knees, but at length they managed to get a sense of direction and pushed on against the blizzard. Now and again it would clear for a moment or two, only to blow the harder afterward. In such a temporary relief, Sundar found they were on the edge of a steep slope and that, 30 feet below them, lay the body of a traveler who had obviously fallen from the path. He asked his companion to clamber with him down the slope to the man's rescue. The Tibetan refused curtly, stating that he wished to get to Ranget in safety, and that if the Christian were fool enough and holy enough to risk his life on the dangerous escarpment, he could do it by himself.

"I shall save *myself*," was the Tibetan's final word.

The sadhu clambered down the mountainside, discovered the fallen man was alive, dragged him to the path, and with the injured man clinging to him, began the slow trek to Ranget, his journey's end. The fallen man was almost frozen to death, and Sundar knew that if they fell both of them would perish in the blizzard. Only by keeping moving could they hope to survive.

Almost within sight of Ranget the blizzard cleared. Both men, revived and clearheaded by their joint exertions, noticed at the same moment a prostrate form. It was the sadhu's earlier companion, lying dead and half-covered by deep snow.

"He that saveth his life shall lose it," murmured the sadhu, "and he that loseth his life for My sake shall find it." As they trudged slowly into Ranget he told the man by his side the wonderful, strange story of Jesus, who had also given His life that others might live.

Whatever Sundar achieved in Tibet, his annual visits there gave him immense fame in India and, far more important to him, stirred the Indian church, slowly becoming aware of its own resources and responsibilities, into new missionary zeal.

In 1917, when he returned, he found letters asking him to visit South India. In 1918 there were urgent requests that he should visit the Far East. He acceded to both requests. In 1919 there were suggestions that he might visit the West—Britain, Europe, and America.

It might well seem that nothing more important could have happened during 1919 than these invitations to visit and preach in the West. The sadhu had often wished to go to Britain and America. But there was no money to pay his fare, and he could not use money lodged in Simla for his Tibetan tours. All he knew was that if God wanted him to go He would provide the means.

Then something very wonderful happened.

Back again from the perils of Tibet, Sundar sat by Sher Singh on the familiar veranda. The moon was brilliant, lighting up the distant trees across the plain. From the town came the sound of a band playing at a wedding. Here and there a jackal howled. Suddenly there was the shriek of an engine's whistle as the night express tore through the moonlight to Ludhiana. Sundar's memory quickened. On just such a night as this, though a colder one, with the whistle sounding in his ears, he had determined to end his life unless he found peace before dawn. On such a night Jesus had come and spoken to him, 15 years earlier.

He started as Sher Singh's hand was stretched out toward him, to clutch his yellow robe. His father's voice brought him swiftly back to the present.

"My son, I too have come to love Jesus."

They talked far into the night. As they were going to bed, Sher Singh stopped and turned.

"My son, if God wants you to go to England and America, I will give the money for your fare. That way I may make amends for my sin."

14

1920-22

The Heathen West

Old Sher Singh's thank offering to God confirmed the sadhu in believing that he should accept the invitations he was receiving to visit the West.

In January 1920 he sailed on the "City of Cairo" for England.

At once it was plain he would be embarrassed by the curiosity of strangers, and in England and America the sensation become more acutely painful. He had not realized how completely alien he would appear. The obvious thing would have been to discard his yellow cloak and wear European dress, but this he steadily refused to do. There was a sense in which he regarded this unending, merciless stare of strangers as a discipline to be endured for the sake of his mission. That he *had* a mission in the West he did not for a moment doubt.

He had hoped to find Britain a Christian country. Instead, he discovered it to be a land where God was forgotten and where the deep-rooted spirituality of the East was replaced by a repellent, relentless materialism. The Continent and Australia he found as bad, and he believed that America was even worse.

First he stayed in Birmingham, moving later to Oxford and London. Wherever he went crowds gathered. His story was written up, not without sympathy and understanding, by the daily press. For a while he succumbed to the pressure of his hosts, and wore Western shoes and an overcoat. Very soon, however, he rejected the coat, declaring that after the bitterness of the Himalayas, Britain was not cold enough for him. Whenever he could conveniently do so, he shunned buses, trains, and trams, for he soon found that the ever-present maelstrom of hurrying, thrusting, grim-visaged people drew even his peaceful spirit toward its vortex. Meditation was difficult. It was hard to realize that these multitudes, who seemed to think of nothing but security, business, and money, could have the same hunger in their souls as his Eastern people.

In America he was bitterly distressed to find, very soon after his arrival, that a publicity campaign was arranged for him during his stay, and he was horrified to discover that its promoters expected to make a great deal of money both for themselves and for him out of his meetings. The scheme had nothing to do with the church, and he was relieved to hand over his arrangements to friends whose only desire was that he might speak the same Good News to America that he carried throughout the East.

The sadhu found he could *not* say the same things in the West.

India was a religious country; the West, it seemed, was utterly indifferent to all spiritual values. His mission was to let them see themselves as he saw them.

Hundreds were deeply offended at what they regarded as the presumption and offensively frank judgments of this 30-year-old "holy man from the Orient," who knew nothing of the stress of industrial life and the tensions of modern business. Thousands, however, who listened, were moved, challenged, and converted by his preaching. He was as fearless in his denunciation as he was tender in his pleading.

"I found a stone in a pool among the Himalayas," he told an audience. "It was hollow, and when I broke it I found the center completely dry. So it is here in the West.

You have lain for centuries in the water of Christianity, but it has never penetrated to your hearts."

No audience could remain unmoved as they looked at the flashing eyes in the olive-skinned, black-bearded face and heard his soft tones harden when he declared: "In the day of judgment the non-Christians of the East will get a lighter sentence than you of the West. They have never heard the gospel. You have had your chance and thrown it away."

He paraphrased the words of Jesus and shocked Americans by asserting that his Master called them: "Come unto Me all ye that are heavy-laden with gold, and I will give you rest."

To the Archbishop of Canterbury he spoke of caste in Hindu India—and of caste and class-consciousness in the Christian Church of the West.

From America he went back to India, touching at Honolulu, Australia, and Ceylon. Wherever he went he said: "My work is to preach." Few who heard him will ever forget him.

He reached India in the late spring and, after a preaching tour of various Christian conferences and retreats, set out for the Himalayas and Tibet. The harshness of the Tibetan Buddhists, the dangers of the Himalayan chasms and snow-bridges were welcome after the spiritual rebuffs he had endured in the West, and it is surprising that he was persuaded to undertake a second European tour within two years.

One of the reasons that swayed his decision was the opportunity of visiting Palestine on his way to England. He had yearned to do this for so long that when the chance came he could not resist it. There were moments when his heart came near to breaking as he made his pilgrimage up the sacred streets and among the holy places of the gospel story.

This time he did not go to America but visited many of the European countries before ending his tour in Britain. France, Switzerland, Norway, Sweden, Denmark, Germany, Holland all honored him, but by the time he reached England it was evident that he was very tired. His main platforms in Britain were those of arranged conferences, and he found himself speaking more often at conventions for the deepening of the spiritual life than to the general public.

The sadhu himself doubted whether he had achieved very much by these visits. Yet the challenge to the Church was tremendous, and his influence on individuals was incalculable. His very appearance gave authority to his words. The servant who opened the front door and ran to tell her mistress that she thought Christ had come to the house and the children who played with him on the hearthrug and afterward wanted Jesus to put them to bed were only expressing in words the thought of all who met him. His Christlike appearance was matched by the gentleness and authority of his bearing and spirit.

15

1922-29

The Flame Burns Down

Some of his friends believed that when the year 1922 ended the sadhu was strangely grieved, that he had wished to die in that year. He was 33. It was at that age that Jesus had died, and the sadhu longed to walk in His steps.

If he did not die, he suffered, for the following year his father died.

About the same time the Alliance Bank of Simla went bankrupt. The funds for his Tibetan tours were lodged there, and it would not be easy to replace them. The loss of money meant little in itself, and his father was already an old man, but these strains were added to the sadhu's tiredness after his European tour. Something of his virility was already gone, and when he consulted a specialist about his eyes, which had begun to trouble him, he was given the dreadful news that one eye was practically useless and the other might become so. He was forced to rest more than ever before, and it became plain that the driving willpower that had kept him going when he was on the move might hardly be enough to sustain him when forced into inactivity.

Despite the failure of the Alliance Bank, enough money was made available for him to begin his annual trek into Tibet the same year. He had not missed this summer tour for 15 years, sometimes breaking across the border in different places during the same year. He had even tried to preach there in winter, but being snowbound for 17 days in a little hut had shown him the folly of spending time there that could be better used elsewhere. In 1923 he carried through his plans, but the following year, when relations were strained between Tibet and the outside world, officials made it impossible for him to cross the frontier. For the first time he was faced with failure. His vitality was ebbing; his doctor warned him not to undertake any long preaching tours in the plains; and he found himself attacked by internal troubles that would not yield to treatment.

Such a state of frustration was almost unendurable.

He had read little, so he always said, but the Bible and the "book of nature." Occasionally, under pressure, he had written a few articles, and some of his addresses had been taken down in shorthand and circulated. The welcome they received and the effect they produced turned the sadhu to the two things he could most easily do in solitude—reading and writing.

Most of his time he spent in his little house in Kotgarh or with his friends at the Leper Hospital in Sabathu. For three years he rested almost continually. His name was as well-known as ever, but most men saw him no more. Instead, they read the books and pamphlets that he sent to the world from Sabathu. The friendship of George Barne, later bishop of Lahore, of C. F. Andrews, of Rev. J. T. Riddle, and of Mr. Watson of the Leper Hospital meant a great deal to him at this period. Many people in India thought only that, like other holy men, he had gone for a while into retirement for refreshment of spirit, and few, even of his intimate friends, realized how ill he was.

The truth was that the flame was burning very low.

In 1927 he announced to Mr. Watson that he intended to resume his preaching within the forbidden frontiers of Tibet. The passes across the mountains were beginning to open, as the swollen, icy waters of the Sutlej proved. The high snows were melting and Tibetan traders, having spent the winter in the warmer Indian plains and hill stations, were planning to return. The sadhu met them in Simla and, as he heard them talk of towns and villages that he knew, monasteries and lamaseries that he had visited, his heart began to throb.

When April came, he caught the train from Sabathu to Kalka and began the long trek up the "Pilgrim Line" that leads from Rishikesh toward the high, mountainous region where pilgrims seek the holy men.

Forty miles beyond Rishikesh, the sadhu's prostrate form was found by the roadside, lying in a pool of blood. He had suffered a sudden hemorrhage of the stomach and had to be carried back to the Simla train by a group of friendly traders.

Those who saw him when he returned to Sabathu shook their heads and declared sadly that he would never again make an attempt on Tibet.

They were wrong.

16

1929

The Last Journey

"*Sadhuji,* you ought never to take the risk! You may never return!"

Sundar made his old reply: "I never expect to return from Tibet!"

He assured his friends that he had made arrangements about his small possessions in case he did not come back, and that most of it was for the help of Christian children, and for the furtherance of Christian missionary work in Tibet.

Some of those to whom he talked in Sabathu reminded him that he had taken no vigorous exercise for months, and that even for a mountaineer in strict training the journey over the 18,000-feet passes would be full of danger.

"I am ready for the journey that I must take," the sadhu replied. Not until the journey was over did they think it a strange reply.

It was April 1929. The sadhu had hardly left Sabathu during the winter, except to share in a conference at Bareilly. Once again the rivers were swollen with the white waters of the melting winter snows. Once more the Tibetan traders were turning homeward for the summer. The pilgrims were gathering at Kalka and along the banks of the Ganges for the first great trek of the year to the holy shrine of Badrinath.

Near Badrinath the road turns off, following the course of the Dauli River until it reaches the Nita Pass, where some Christian families had their homes. Once the "Pilgrim Line" is left at Badrinath, the road becomes a mountain track, rising eventually to almost 20,000 feet. Immense rocks overhang the narrow trail, and on the other side precipices drop sheer for thousands of feet. From these narrow paths many a pony and hillman falls screaming to his death during the summer. Snow- and ice-bridges span the chasms and, now and again, two or three pine logs take the place of a broken bridge. They are neither supported below nor fixed together at the end, and may be thrown across a gap 50 feet wide, while a roaring cataract whips up icy spray 500 feet below.

The unending snow, close at hand and on the distant ranges, is glaring and dazzling, so that it is sometimes not possible to see the track clearly until the eyes have been rested.

On April 13 the tall figure of the sadhu came up through the trees toward the gate of the Leper Hospital. With him was Sunnu Lal, the Indian preacher engaged in leprosy work. They shook hands with Mr. Watson, the superintendent of the home, at the entrance to the compound. The sadhu was wearing his dark glare glasses, carrying a staff, and was without sandals. He and Sunnu Lal went down the hill toward Kalka, the little town where the plains meet the hills and the railway, leaves for Rishikesh, the beginning of the "Pilgrim Line."

No one noticed the sadhu after he left Kalka, though he should have been conspicuous enough with his saffron robe and dark glasses. None of the pilgrim record books along the road were signed with his name. There were no police reports of anything happening to him on the well frequented "Pilgrim Line" to Badrinath. The Christian families near Mansorowar Lake, in the Kailas Mountains, had no news of him. But it was not until the end of June, when he had told his friends that he would probably be back, that anyone began to be unduly anxious about him.

By that time it was too late to worry and too late even to inquire.

All trace of the sadhu was gone.

He never came back.

Thousands of his fellow Christians believed that he had joined the hermits in the Kailas Ranges, but he had never sought that type of solitary existence. Others believed that he had succeeded in entering Tibet and been martyred there at last, like his countryman, Kartar Singh.

Those who knew him best and had seen him last thought of his precarious health, of his previous collapse, of his partly blind eyes. They remembered the precipitous climbs, the yawning gaps where the bridges should have been. They recalled his own words, his readiness for death, his preparations in case he never returned.

They knew what had happened.

They knew that the man in the saffron robe, the man who loved and changed India, the man who had disappeared, would never come back.

His death added one more mystery to a life that few people completely understood. Those who believed he would one day descend from his mountain fastnesses were proved wrong. Among the ranges he crossed so often there stands no memorial to his name. In time even his legend may be largely forgotten. Yet those who knew him best were right when they said that he was not dead. His spirit lives on in the church in north India, which he quickened to a new sense of unity, responsibility, and adventure, and those who one day write the story of that church will find his memorial in the changed lives, the leadership, and the service of innumerable men and women to whom he was the voice of God.

Epilogue

There is a message for present-day Christians in the life of Sadhu Sundar Singh. It is possible for us to finish the life story of this saint of God and miss the impact and the challenge found there. The sadhu's life was so unusual and his walk with God so intimate that we are in danger of looking upon this saintly follower of the Lord as a character out of history. Actually, born in 1889, his adult life was contemporary with our forebears in the emerging American holiness movement of the early 20th century.

His life of devotion and determined freedom from the impediments of materialistic handicaps parallels the lives of St. Augustine and St. Francis of Assisi, who lived seven centuries earlier. Like them, Sundar was a mystic who spent hours in contemplation and in converse with the Christ whom he adored. But again, like the two Early Church saints, he was imbued with a compassionate spirit and a driving compulsion to proclaim the truth of God and to alleviate the physical suffering of helpless humanity. Sundar Singh could not disassociate himself from the spiritual and physical needs of those for whom his Christ suffered and died.

The motivating factor in Sundar's plan of life was to follow his Master as closely as was physically possible. That being the case, he could do naught but minister to the bodies and the souls of his fellowmen. It was not possible for him to withdraw in isolated contemplation and prayer, but rather to go and seek out the lost.

So, homeless, friendless, and practically penniless, he turned his back on his ancestral home, with its comforts, prestige, and all that most men count worthwhile. With what depth of feeling he could have sung,

Jesus! I my cross have taken,
All to leave and follow Thee;
Naked, poor, despised, forsaken,
Thou from hence my all shalt be.

In the sadhu's estimation there was no one too sinful for Christ to forgive, no one fallen so low but that Christ could restore him, no man so lost but that God would not only welcome him home but would see him coming afar off and run to meet him with outstretched arms.

He had no wish to live as an ascetic, inflicting punishment upon himself and courting suffering as a means of earning favor with God. He endured trials of soul-searing intensity, accepted physical deprivation and persecution, in all of which he endured as seeing Him who is invisible. An ascetic makes a virtue of his suffering. The sadhu met affliction and opposition with abounding joy as he walked in companionship with his Lord, who had no place to lay His head, though the beasts of the field had dens and the birds of the air had nests. Sundar's self-imposed life of an itinerant holy man was to him not arduous; rather it brought him the peace and joy and the fellowship with Christ that had so long eluded him.

Of sadhus, India had many. Some were sincere; many were frauds. Hundreds of the holy men were victims of the same delusion that induces many in this enlightened day to seek merit in God's sight by good works, by deeds of benevolence and mercy, and by abstention from certain foods at given periods of time. Darkness of soul and ignorance of God's plan of salvation are not dispelled by civilization or culture. The light of God's truth is revealed through His Word, in the message of a preacher, and by the faithful testimony of one whose eyes have been opened and whose soul is redeemed. How diligent we should be in our witnessing, for hungry hearts are always nearby, needy souls are at our elbows, living next door, or just around the corner!

The story of Sadhu Sundar Singh would not be complete without paying tribute to his mother, who in her sphere was as remarkable as the son who adored her. We think of the women in India as downgraded, subservient, and with one primary purpose—to please their husbands. Such was not the case in a Sikh household, where the mother is respected by her husband and honored by her children. This was especially true in the home of Sirdar Sher Singh, Sundar's father.

Although not a Christian, Sundar's mother was devoted to her religious faith. She paid reverence to the spiritual leaders among the Sikhs and Hindus alike. And she offered hospitality to the Christian ladies of the missionary settlement nearby. Throughout the entire community she was known for her religious devotion and purity of character.

Long hours were given each day to prayer and religious instruction by this devoted mother. Her own private devotions were taken care of upon rising long before dawn. She would take the ceremonial bath and then carry a flower offering to the temple. Each daily act would be dedicated in some special way to God. At the end of the day she would once more carry out her ritual of prayer and worship before retiring. More than that, on certain days she would go without food in order that her prayers might be more earnest and acceptable to God.

In later years Sundar said, "It was the Holy Spirit who made me a Christian, but it was my mother who made me a sadhu." It is easy to understand how this deeply religious woman would influence her son's highly imaginative nature and prepare him for his commitment to the Christian faith.

A glimpse of the religious atmosphere and rare quality of life in this home is afforded in the following comment the sadhu made concerning his sister: "My sister woke each morning at early dawn to perform her devotions and to keep her religious observances." He went on to compare her to some in Christian homes "who spend five minutes in devotions and then are tired, but who hope to spend all eternity in praising God."

No transition from darkness to dawn, from antagonism to acceptance, could be more revolutionary than was that of Sundar Singh. The rebellious youth who tore the pages from his New Testament and cast them into the fire and who joined other lads in throwing stones and mud at the Christian missionaries became the humble follower of the Master. He answered his Lord's call without reservations, turning his back on wealth, prestige, comforts, family, to wander as a pilgrim preacher, walking barefooted from village to village, without money, clothed in the single yellow saffron robe that designated him as a sadhu or holy man.

His appeal to India was irresistible. The extent of his influence will not be known until the records are opened at that great day when all persons shall be rewarded according to their deeds.

There are those who claim that the Beatitudes and the noble standards of the New Testament are not relevant to today's way of life. Sundar's faith enabled him to take the Bible literally and to put into practice the standards taught and exemplified by the Master. The results of such a life are inevitable. Time and time again, those who were deeply enmeshed in superstition and a religion of works were won to the Christ, "who, when he was reviled, reviled not again; when he suffered, he threatened not; but committed himself to him that judgeth righteously" (1 Pet. 2:23). All of which emphasizes the truth that Christian deeds are far more effective than any defense of doctrine.

Important Dates

1889:   Born at Rampur, Punjab.

1903:   His mother dies. December—conversion.

1904:   Outcaste. To school in Ludhiana.

1905:   Baptized in Simla; becomes a sadhu.

1906:   First long tour of the north; meets Stokes.

1907:   Works with Stokes in hills; in leprosy hospital at Sabathu and in plague camps at Lahore.

1908:   First visit to Tibet (continued throughout his life).

1909:   St. John's Divinity College, Lahore.

1911:   Returns preaching license and returns to sadhu's life.

1912:   Increased touring throughout north India and Buddhist states. Finds Maharishi of Kailas and meets the Sannyasi Mission.
Attempts to become padre to British Columbian Sikhs. The fast.

1918:   Visit to south India and Ceylon.

1919:   Tour of Burma, Malaya, China, and Japan.

1920:   First visit to Britain, America, and Australia.

1922:   Second European tour. Returns to protracted series of Indian retreats and conferences.

1923:   Failure of Alliance Bank. Turned back from Tibet. Physical condition deteriorates.

1925-27:   Leads quiet life in Simla Hills, doing literary work.

1927:   Fails to reach Tibetan border owing to illness.

1929:   The last attempt on Tibet.

1933:   Probate of his will granted and government of India assumes him to be dead.